Walker Gibson

Seeing and Writing

Fifteen Exercises in Composing Experience

Second Edition

David McKay Company, Inc.
New York

No method nor discipline can supersede the necessity of being forever on the alert. What is a course of history, or philosophy, or poetry, or the most admirable routine of life, compared with the discipline of looking always at what is to be seen? Will you be a reader, a student merely, or a seer? Read your fate, see what is before you, and walk on into futurity.

THOREAU

Preface

This is a book of fifteen exercises in writing for college students. Its assumption is that if young writers are encouraged to look hard at their own experience they will see something there and say something about it of interest to their teachers. It may be that teachers of college composition who are bored by their students' writing deserve what they get. This book proposes that students can be so directed to express themselves that they will inform, entertain, and instruct their instructors.

A liberally educated man is a talker and a writer, a composer of words. He is a man who can change his voice without losing track of himself: for him the terms of the historian and the scientist and the poet are all available ways of ordering a world, and their variety does not frighten him. In this book a systematic attempt is made to place the student in positions where he must see his experience from shifting points of view, and must change his terms and his tone of voice as he does so. That such an effort may lead to the student's "finding himself" is a promise that probably no teacher should make, though it is worth repeating here that most of us find ourselves only after we have spent some time getting lost first.

The liberally educated man, moreover, knows his limits. He knows, for example, that the words he uses are not identical with the things he sees, and he writes accordingly with modesty, good humor, and careful courage—in other words, with *style*. "It is style," Robert Oppenheimer has written, "which complements affirmation with limitation and with humility; it is style which makes it possible to act effectively, but not absolutely; it is style which enables us to find a harmony between the pursuit of ends essential to us, and a regard for the views, the sensibilities, the aspirations of those to whom the problem may appear in another light; it is style which is the deference that action pays to uncertainty; it is above all style through which power defers to reason." One purpose of this book is to encourage in the student some uses of style, however humble, in that sense.

The first edition of this book appeared almost fifteen years ago, and it is sobering to reflect on how much has happened in those years. For one obvious thing, college students' attitudes toward their teachers and their education have become less trustful, with consequences both good and bad. In this new edition, the student is invited to challenge his education from several points of view, with the help of some recent attacks on the school room. Other changes in this edition include fresh materials for about one third of the text. But the essential structure of the original work still seems, to its creator, sound enough: that is, to see and resee one's immediate experience by the trying-on of new language.

And that structure is easily summarized in an order of exercises. The first four chapters explore acts of "seeing" one's ordinary day-to-day experience. Chapter 1 invites the traditional description of the college campus, with a focus on some detail seen as significant. Ellison's exemplary description from *Invisible Man* suggests the ambiguity that can complicate any effort to give significance to things, and chapter 2, with accompanying illustrations and experiments from a recent *Scientific American*, raises the whole question of visual ambiguity. The aim here is to cast a little healthy doubt on the assumptions we make about what we see and the World Out There. Seeing is believing? Chapter 3 makes the point that visual seeing is itself a kind of prejudicial medium, and that the blind person in particular can be conscious of another world altogether. In chapter 4, turning in a more positive direction, effective seeing is defined as "reading" the environment, interpreting details in some purposeful way, just as Mark Twain learned to read the Mississippi River.

Chapters 5 through 8 ask the student to see his own education, with the hope that the passages for reading may offer him fresh terms with which to see himself anew. From the poignant drama of Kazin's schooldays in Brownsville to the wide-open euphoria of Consciousness III, the student is provided with a variety of vocabularies to help him face an important question: How do I see myself as a student?

The remaining chapters follow the pattern of the first edition, focusing on the writer as student-historian and then as student-scientist. Chapter 9 asks for a simple description of a building—the façade of a neighborhood church. Chapter 10 requires a new look at this façade with a historian's metaphors, while in chapter 11 the student must examine critically his own historical assumptions. For chapter 12 the student writes an impressionistic report of the wind; for chapter 13 he sees his wind new, in statistical terms, by experimenting with a homemade anemometer that he constructs himself; and in chapter 14 he faces the limitations of his own "human standpoint" as a measurer of nature. In the final exercise certain aspects of the writer's problem are summarized by way of philosophical implications in modern physics, and the student is asked to resee in this light his own activity as a composer of essays.

Passages for reading have been kept brief. In most cases they precede the directions for writing, their purpose being to introduce various terms and points of view for the information and encouragement of the student. But in no sense is Imitation of Great Writers intended. There is no thought that after reading Mark Twain on the Mississippi, the student should write like Mark Twain—except that he should see his own Mississippi in his own backyard.

Some observations of a practical sort are due the prospective teacher. The intention is that each of these exercises might represent part of one week's work in a composition course, together with whatever lessons in rhetoric, supplementary reading, use of the library, and so on the teacher may wish to assign. But the weekly essay is by no means the only appropriate schedule, and the work might properly go either faster or slower. The series can probably be completed comfortably in one semester, with essays of perhaps five hundred words each. But it is quite conceivable that a teacher might wish to handle the material more deliberately, with additional reading, perhaps requiring papers of greater length. By and large it would seem best to offer the exercises in an order close to the one given, though this too need not be inflexible. It is particularly important that no new essay should be assigned until the previous one has been discussed and returned to the student.

The choice of reading passages is, of course, one man's choice; the list can certainly be improved by each teacher's ingenuity as his needs suggest. Each selection moreover can be approached in a number of ways that differ from the one suggested in the text, and the essentially empirical character of these assignments generally should not discourage the teacher from considering the literary or aesthetic aspects of the material if he so desires. The teacher's own resourcefulness in response to his local situation is especially necessary in the assignments on the language of history (chapters 10–11) and the language of science (chapters 13–14). Here there is an opportunity to make some contact between the student's English class and his other courses, and, if these exercises can involve relevant selections from the student's own textbooks in history and science, so much the better. It is always a pleasant surprise when the words of one course can make sense in another.

In any case it seems to the compiler improbable that any one teacher would wish to pursue the precise pattern laid out in this book for longer than two or three years consecutively, assuming he could abide it that long. After such a period, it's to be hoped, he would want to apply some of the techniques exemplified here to his own materials, with his own emphasis.

I have spoken of the book's "precise pattern" and its "systematic attempt." These do not appear to be the phrases of student-centered, open-ended education now so much in vogue. There may indeed be something charmingly old-fashioned in any effort to invite students to perform certain actions in a certain order. As any reader can see, there is enormous room for varied and independent responses in these exercises, but it remains a fact that the exercises start somewhere, proceed in certain directions, and purport to end somewhere else. If this be blasphemy . . .

In the earlier edition I mentioned my debt to the English department at Amherst College, and particularly to Professor Theodore Baird, for having taught me much of what I thought I knew about composition. That debt is still real, though my years since then have been spent at two very different institutions with different kinds of clientele—New York University and the University of Massachusetts. Inevitably these years have left their footnotes on my attitudes toward students and teaching. Still, any teacher who used and enjoyed *Seeing and Writing* in its earlier form will find here a familiar shape which I hope may be enjoyable (or even useful) again.

W.G.

Contents

The most obvious aspect of the field of actual experience is its disorderly character. To grasp this fundamental truth is the first step in wisdom.

Chapter
1
Seeing
a Campus

What do you want to accomplish as a writer, as a student of writing in a composition course? You might try to list some of your aims. For example, you might say that you want to convey your thoughts to others through a skillful use of words. You want to communicate clearly so that other people will really grasp your meaning. You want to express yourself accurately, vividly. These are reasonable aims, you might say, for a course in composition.

But as a matter of fact they are not reasonable at all—they are impossible. Consider your own thoughts, for instance, and your desire to convey them to others. What *are* your thoughts? Think about your own thinking for a moment—think about your own thinking right *now*. What is in your mind? You are sitting in a chair, probably, just slightly aware of its touch on you, just slightly aware that it is or isn't upholstered. You are aware of being alone (or not alone), of the time, the temperature, the state of your stomach. How many thoughts are competing in your head, now that you think of them? A date, a game, the shape of this sentence, sleepiness, anxiety, boredom. Life! The more you think about your thinking, the more it's a

1

mess. And if you ask yourself, now, what has happened to the state of your mind since you started thinking about it like this, your answer would have to be that it has certainly changed by the very process of trying to express it. Were you really aware of your hunger a minute ago, or is it just that you are now being reminded of it? The more we try to describe our thoughts at a given moment, the more we do them an injustice by that very effort.

The state of our minds, as it really is at this moment, is inexpressible, and we can't "convey" that state to anybody, not even to ourselves.

Well, then, what *is* expressible? It would be possible to say, in answer to that question, that strictly speaking nothing is, that no idea can be "conveyed" precisely from the mind of one person to the mind of another. Yet we need only look around us to admire the proofs of some kind of communicating going on in the world. The business of the day gets done, on the whole marvelously well. Airplanes take off, often on time, and they land safely in dense fog without ever seeing the ground. Someone has been talking to someone else, and, if he has not expressed the state of his thoughts, he has at least gotten something done. A man in the dark, watching the pips on a radar screen, tells the pilot that he should lower his wheels, that he is nearing the runway, that he is all right—and this miracle of communication is enough to silence any skepticism.

But the practical question that confronts us in the situation of the composition class is still unanswered. What shall we write about? If we can't convey "ourselves" and the state of our minds, and if we aren't landing planes in a fog, what alternatives do we have in our search for useful problems of communication? What area of experience can we examine as a fruitful and controllable field for expression?

There are probably many answers to this question: the one adopted by this book is an obvious one. It proposes that we begin by *looking* at something familiar and ready at hand—your college campus. What do we do in the face of a scene that stands before our eyes; how do we render an experience of this thing in words? What do we choose to look at? What do we consider important or significant? Those are some of the problems presented by your first essay.

Directions for Essay 1

Write a short description of your college campus, in which you focus on one particular scene in detail that seems to represent or express for you your feelings about your campus.

Now here is a short passage from a novel in which a fine contemporary writer, Ralph Ellison, dramatizes a character looking back nostalgically on his college campus. This is an intense and lyrical piece of writing, and it probably doesn't express attitudes *you* feel about your campus. Nor is this particular campus (modeled on Tuskegee Institute in Alabama) probably much like your campus in appearance and atmosphere. Nevertheless, here is a bit of literature on our subject that ought to be inspirational, and it focuses, like your own description, on a detail that is seen as particularly significant. (Note the third paragraph on the "Founder's" statue.) We will have more to say about that significance later.

FROM *Invisible Man*

RALPH ELLISON

It was a beautiful college. The buildings were old and covered with vines and the roads gracefully winding, lined

From *Invisible Man*, Copyright 1952, by Ralph Ellison. Reprinted by permission of Random House, Inc.

with hedges and wild roses that dazzled the eyes in the summer sun. Honeysuckle and purple wisteria hung heavy from the trees and white magnolias mixed with their scents in the bee-humming air. I've recalled it often . . . : How the grass turned green in the springtime and how the mocking birds fluttered their tails and sang, how the moon shone down on the buildings, how the bell in the chapel tower rang out the precious short-lived hours; how the girls in bright summer dresses promenaded the grassy lawn. Many times . . . I've closed my eyes and walked along the forbidden road that winds past the girls' dormitories, past the hall with the clock in the tower, its windows warmly aglow, on down past the small white Home Economics practice cottage, whiter still in the moonlight, and on down the road with its sloping and turning, paralleling the black powerhouse with its engines droning earthshaking rhythms in the dark, its windows red from the glow of the furnace, on to where the road became a bridge over a dry riverbed, tangled with brush and clinging vines; the bridge of rustic logs, made for trysting, but virginal and untested by lovers; on up the road, past the buildings, with the southern verandas half-a-city-block long, to the sudden forking, barren of buildings, birds, or grass, where the road turned off to the insane asylum.

I always come this far and open my eyes. The spell breaks and I try to resee the rabbits, so tame through having never been hunted, that played in the hedges and along the road. And I see the purple and silver of thistle growing between the broken glass and sunheated stones, the ants moving nervously in single file, and I turn and retrace my steps and come back to the winding road past the hospital, where at night in certain wards the gay student nurses dispensed a far more precious thing than pills to lucky boys in the know; and I come to a stop at the chapel. And then it is suddenly winter, with the moon high above and the chimes in the steeple ringing and a sonorous choir of trombones rendering a Christmas carol; and over all is a quietness and an ache as though all the world were loneliness. And I stand and listen beneath the high-hung moon, hearing "A Mighty Fortress Is Our God," majestically mellow on four trombones, and then the organ. The sound floats over all, clear like the night, liquid, serene, and lonely. And I stand as for an answer and see in my mind's eye the cabins surrounded by empty fields beyond red clay roads, and beyond a certain road a river, sluggish and covered with algae more yellow than green in its stagnant stillness; past more empty fields, to the sun-shrunk shacks at the railroad crossing where the disabled veterans visited the whores, hobbling down the tracks on crutches and canes; sometimes pushing the legless, thighless one in a red wheelchair. And sometimes I listen to hear if music reaches that far, but recall only the drunken laughter of sad, sad whores. And I stand in the circle where three roads converge near the statue, where we drilled four-abreast down the smooth asphalt and pivoted and entered the chapel on Sundays, our uniforms pressed, shoes shined, minds laced up, eyes blind like those of robots to visitors and officials on the low, whitewashed reviewing stand.

. . . Then in my mind's eye I see the bronze statue of the college Founder, the cold Father symbol, his hands outstretched in the breathtaking gesture of lifting a veil that flutters in hard, metallic folds above the face of a kneeling slave; and I am standing puzzled, unable to decide whether the veil is really being lifted, or lowered more firmly in place; whether I am witnessing a revelation or a more efficient blinding. And as I gaze, there is a rustle of wings and I see a flock of starlings flighting before me and, when I look again, the bronze face, whose empty eyes look upon a world I have never seen, runs with liquid chalk—creating another ambiguity to puzzle my groping mind: Why is a bird-soiled statue more commanding than one that is clean?

Oh, long green stretch of campus, Oh, quiet songs at dusk, Oh, moon that kissed the steeple and flooded the perfumed nights, Oh, bugle that called in the morning, Oh, drum that marched us militarily at noon—what was real,

what solid, what more than a pleasant, time-killing dream?
. . . If real, why is it that I can recall in all that island of
greenness no fountain but one that was broken, corroded and
dry? And why does no rain fall through my recollections,
sound through my memories, soak through the hard dry crust
of the still so recent past? Why do I recall, instead of the odor
of seed bursting in springtime, only the yellow contents of the
cistern spread over the lawn's dead grass? Why? And how?
How and why?

Obviously, one man's campus is not another man's. Here
are some sentences from a recent Tuskegee catalogue, just to
taste the available variety:

Tuskegee Profile

Tuskegee Institute is a co-educational, privately
controlled, professional, scientific, and technical institution,
with regional accreditation from the Southern Association of
Colleges and Schools, and with specialized approval for
several of its programs—nursing, dietetics, veterinary medi-
cine, and teacher education—from their respective national
professional associations. This non-sectarian, independent institution—founded by Booker T. Washington in 1881—is
located in Tuskegee Institute, Alabama, one mile west of the
town of Tuskegee—which can be reached via three U.S.
Highways, 80, 29, and Interstate 85. . . .

Special features in Tuskegee's program include: The
George Washington Carver Museum (named for the distinguished scientist who worked at Tuskegee) which preserves the

tools and handiworks of Dr. Carver, as well as houses displays on Tuskegee, Africa, and Negro life in general; the George Washington Carver Research Foundation, center for a variety of research sponsored by government agencies and private industry; the fully accredited 160 bed John A. Andrew Hospital, which provides general health services for the community and specialized care for some patients from outlying areas; the Tuskegee Archives, a chief center for information on the problems and history of the Negro since 1896; and the Reserve Officers Training Corps for the Army and Air Force; and the Human Resources Development Center, a nucleus for continuing adult education.

Tuskegee employs approximately 925 personnel (about 25 percent faculty and approximately 75 percent staff). Physical facilities, including 5,189 acres of land and more than 150 major buildings, are valued in excess of $30,000,000. The school's present endowment and certain reserve funds are in excess of $14,000,000. The Institute is now engaged in a multimillion dollar development program to provide increasing academic excellence and superior quality in its programs and services.

Are these sentences from the college catalogue any more accurate, or less accurate, than Ellison's poetic description? Which is closer to the "real" Tuskegee? Those are questions which are probably not worth asking. Instead, to account for the differences we have to ask questions about the *acts of writing*, the circumstances, purposes, and implied audiences. Ellison's description is of course highly personal, filled with emotional memories of specific places and events. It is part of a novel, remember, and in the context of the whole novel it is filled with irony, for the hero-narrator learns to look on his college years as absurdly comical, even contemptible. In any case the novelist's tone of voice would hardly do for the opening page of a college catalogue, where the style is exceedingly impersonal, concerned with generalizations and factual data rather than individual details. What is wanted in the catalogue is a dignified statement of academic excellence, aimed at prospective students and others. Think of the difference between saying it is an "institution with regional accreditation" and "it was a beautiful college." The two "its" in that sentence are worlds apart; they point to contrasting acts of selection and expression on the part of the two writers. You can find other parallels and differences, for example, in the references to ROTC training.

Your own style, as you composed essay 1, was probably closer to Ellison's than to the college catalogue's, but the point is, it was your own, and you adopted it in accordance with your own view of yourself as a writer in your particular situation. You made decisions, consciously or not, about your purpose and your reader, and the point of view you might appropriately adopt. These decisions helped you to select, out of the mass of sensations making up your experience of the campus, those details you elected to describe. You certainly did not, and could not, "convey" from your mind to your reader's mind exactly how you see your campus, much less how you feel about it, though presumably you made a good try.

A college campus is one thing—that acreage, those trees and buildings out there. Your description of the campus is something else—*your* creation of a scene and its significance for you. Significance has to come from human interpretation; it's not *in* the objects observed. And so you brought to your scene whatever meaning you wanted your reader to share.

In the case of the passage from *Invisible Man*, the handling of an observed detail is particularly worth your attention. You'll note that as Ellison—or rather, the narrator of the novel—speculates on the significance of the Founder's statue, he confesses he is "puzzled." He isn't sure, he says, whether the Founder is lifting the veil from the face of the kneeling slave, or lowering it over him, consigning him to further darkness. This passage happens to be based on an actual statue of Booker T. Washington, the "founder" of Tuskegee Institute. Here is a photograph of that statue as it stands to this day on the Tuskegee campus.

As you examine that photograph, you have little doubt about the intent of the sculptor. He expected us to see

TUSKEGEE INSTITUTE

Washington in his heroic role as great educator and liberator of Afro-American minds. But Ellison has chosen to see the statue in a double way. Perhaps, he suggests, Washington is "really" lowering the veil right over the poor slave's face. And you can perceive how it might be possible to "see" the statue that way. (It's worth adding that many contemporary black intellectuals now think of Booker T. Washington as the foremost Uncle Tom of his day.)

Ellison, then, chooses to see double in order to make that statue significant for himself and his reader. It is, to use his word, an experience of "ambiguity."

As a matter of fact, ambiguity, seeing double (or triple or quadruple) is a persistent factor in seeing and writing. We choose among competing "versions" of what we see in order to make sense out of our observations. These choices are often hard to make, and we are responsible for them, once they are made. The things we look at will rarely tell us how to interpret, to value, to make significant. We have to do all that ourselves, and live with the consequences.

In the next chapter, we will be making the point that the problem of ambiguity and choice is with us even in "simpler" acts of visual observation. Our eye itself sometimes gives us ambiguous messages.

I began to wonder at about this time just what one saw when one looked at anything really looked at anything.

GERTRUDE STEIN

Chapter
2
Seeing
as Ambiguity

To see, then, is to interpret, to create meaning. It is more than simply a matter of registering messages from the visual nerves. In this chapter, we are going to pause to examine those very messages, for it appears that our visual processes themselves may be called acts of interpretation, even though we are not aware of them. Most of us assume that the raw data we take in visually, images on the retina, represent direct and accurate information about Things Out There. Not so, according to current scientific theory. Our brains are so structured that we inevitably "process" or edit the data our nerves receive, for only then can we make use of it, make sense of it. A recent study asserts that "information about the world enters the mind not as raw data but as highly abstract structures that are the result of a preconscious set of step-by-step transformations of the sensory input. Each transformation step involves the selective destruction of information, according to a program that preexists in the brain. Any set of primary sense data becomes meaningful only after a series of such operations performed on it has transformed the data set into a pattern that matches preexisting mental structure." *

* Gunther S. Stent, "Cellular Communication," *Scientific American* 227, no. 3 (September 1972): 50–51.

You may find that argument hard to follow, and no wonder. If our eyes and brains are all we have to see with, and if it turns out that these organs "transform" reality without our even being aware of it, how are we ever going to get in touch with True Reality at all? The answer to that seems to be that we aren't going to be able to do any such thing, and we'd better adjust to our limited human condition.

This is not the place, you'll be relieved to hear, for a full-dress scientific scrutiny of the limits of perception. But we can at least play some games with our eyesight, and possibly learn a little wholesome modesty about our own processes of perceiving things. The article that follows, while it is to be sure a serious piece of research from a scientific journal, concerns itself particularly with those puzzles and tricks of perception that have entertained people for centuries. The conscious ambiguity that we observed in Ellison's interpretation of the statue becomes here, in these special situations, an unconscious ambiguity built into the very act of seeing with our eyes. Perhaps, as the author suggests, these puzzles may be worth our attention not only for their capacity to amuse, but "for what they can tell us about the nature of the perceptual system."

Multistability in Perception
FRED ATTNEAVE

Pictures and geometric figures that spontaneously change in appearance have a peculiar fascination. A classic example is the line drawing of a transparent cube on page 25. When you first look at the cube, one of its faces seems to be at the front and the other at the back. Then if you look steadily at the drawing for a while, it will suddenly reverse in depth and what was the back face now is the front one. The two orientations will alternate spontaneously; sometimes one is seen, sometimes the other, but never both at once.

When we look steadily at a picture or a geometric figure, the information received by the retina of the eye is relatively constant and what the brain perceives usually does not change. If the figure we are viewing happens to be an ambiguous figure, what the brain perceives may change swiftly without any change in the message it is receiving from the eye. The psychologist is interested in these perceptual alternations not as a curiosity but for what they can tell us about the nature of the perceptual system.

It is the business of the brain to represent the outside world. Perceiving is not just sensing but rather an effect of sensory input on the representational system. An ambiguous figure provides the viewer with an input for which there are two or more possible representations that are quite different and about equally good, by whatever criteria the perceptual system employs. When alternative representations or descriptions of the input are equally good, the perceptual system will sometimes adopt one and sometimes another. In other words, the perception is multistable. There are a number of physical systems that have the same kind of multistable characteristics, and a comparison of multistability in physical and perceptual situations may yield some significant clues to the basic processes of perception. First, however, let us consider several kinds of situations that produce perceptual multistability.

Figure-ground reversal has long been used in puzzle pictures. It is often illustrated by a drawing that can be seen as either a goblet or a pair of faces [*see fig. 1*]. This figure was introduced by the Danish psychologist Edgar Rubin. Many of the drawings and etchings of the Dutch artist Maurits C. Escher are particularly elegant examples of figure-ground

Figure 1–*Reversible Goblet* was introduced by Edgar Rubin in 1915 and is still a favorite demonstration of figure-ground reversal. Either a goblet or a pair of silhouetted faces is seen.

reversal [*see fig. 2*]. These examples are somewhat misleading because they suggest that the components of a figure-ground reversal must be familiar objects. Actually you can make a perfectly good reversing figure by scribbling a meaningless line down the middle of a circle. The line will be seen as a contour or a boundary, and its appearance is quite different depending on which side of the contour is seen as the inside and which as the outside [*see fig. 3*]. The difference is so fundamental that if a person first sees one side of the contour as the object or figure, the probability of his recognizing the same contour when it is shown as part of the other half of the field is little better than if he had never seen it at all; this was demonstrated by Rubin in a classic study of the figure-ground dichotomy.

Note that it is quite impossible to see both sides of the

Figure 2–*Woodcut* by Maurits C. Escher titled "Circle Limit IV (Heaven and Hell)" is a striking example of both figure-ground reversal and competition between rival-object schemata. Devils and angels alternate repeatedly but neither seems to be able to overpower the other.

contour as figures at the same time. Trying to think of the halves as two pieces of a jigsaw puzzle that fit together does not help; the pieces are still seen alternately and not simultaneously. What seems to be involved here is an attribution of surface properties to some parts of a field but not to others. This kind of distinction is of central importance in the problem of scene analysis that Marvin Lee Minsky of the Massachusetts Institute of Technology and other investigators

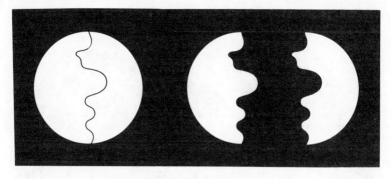

Figure 3–*Reversing Figure* can be made by scribbling a line through a circle. The shape of the contour formed depends on which side of the line is regarded as part of the figure.

of computer simulation have been grappling with lately. The figure made by drawing a line through a circle is actually tristable rather than bistable; the third possibility is being able to see the line as a thing in itself, as a twisted wire rather than the boundary of a figure.

The point of basic interest in figure-ground reversal is that one line can have two shapes. Since an artist's line drawing is readily identifiable with the object it is supposed to portray, and since a shape has much the same appearance whether it is white on black, black on white or otherwise colored, many workers have suggested that the visual system represents or encodes objects primarily in terms of their contours. As we have seen, however, a contour can be part of two shapes. The perceptual representation of a contour is specific to which side is regarded as the figure and which as the ground. Shape may be invariant over a black-white reversal, but it is not invariant over an inside-outside reversal.

Under natural conditions many factors cooperate to determine the figure-ground relationship, and ambiguity is rare. For example, if one area encloses another, the enclosed area is likely to be seen as the figure. If a figure is divided into two areas, the smaller of the areas is favored as the figure [*see fig. 4*].

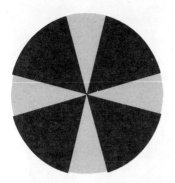 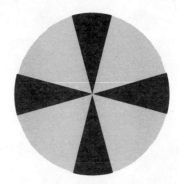

Figure 4–*Larger Area* of a figure is more likely to be seen as the background. Either the large crosses or the small ones may be seen as the figure, but the small crosses have the advantage.

The visual field usually consists of many objects that overlap and occlude one another. The perceptual system has an impressive ability to segregate and sort such objects from one another. Along with distinguishing figure from ground, the system must group the fragments of visual information it receives into separate sets that correspond to real objects. Elements that are close to one another or alike or homogeneous in certain respects tend to be grouped together. When alternative groupings are about equally good, ambiguity results.

For example, if a set of dots are aligned [*see fig. 6*], the perceptual system tends to group them on the basis of this regularity. When the dots are in regular rows and columns, they will be seen as rows if the vertical distance between the dots is greater than the horizontal distance, and they will seem to be in columns if the horizontal distance is greater than the vertical distance. When the spacing both ways is the

Figure 5–*Reversal and Rotation* occur simultaneously in this ingenious design. When the stylized maple-leaf pattern alternates between black and white, it also rotates 90 degrees.

same, the two groupings—rows and columns—tend to alternate. What is interesting and rather puzzling about the situation is that vertical and horizontal groupings are competitive at all. Geometrically the dots form both rows and columns; why, then, does seeing them in rows preclude seeing them in columns at the same moment? Whatever the reason is in terms of perceptual mechanisms, the principle involved appears to be a general one: When elements are grouped

Figure 6–*Aligned Dots* fall into a regular pattern when viewed. Depending on the spacing, dots can be seen as columns (top) or as rows (middle). When vertical and horizontal spacing are equal, dots can be seen as rows or columns but not as both at the same time.

perceptually, they are partitioned; they are not simultaneously cross-classified.

A related case of multistability involves apparent movement. Four lights are arranged in a square so that the diagonally opposite pairs of lights flash simultaneously. If the two diagonal pairs of lights are flashed alternately, it will appear to an observer as if the lights are moving. The apparent motion can take either of two forms: the observer will see motion along the vertical sides of the square, with two pairs of lights, one on the left and the other on the right, moving in opposite directions up and down, or he will see two sets of lights moving back and forth horizontally in opposite directions. If he continues to watch for a while, the motion will switch from vertical to horizontal and vice versa. When one apparent motion gives way to the other, the two perceptions are subjectively so different that the unsuspecting observer is likely to believe there has been some physical change. Apparent movement involves the grouping of events that are separated in both space and time, but the events so grouped are represented as having a common identity; specifically it appears that the same light has moved to a new place. The rivalry between the horizontal and the vertical movement is thus easier to comprehend than the rivalry between rows and columns of dots: if the representational system reflects the laws of the world it represents, the same object cannot traverse two different paths simultaneously or occupy two different places at once.

Ambiguities of grouping are also evident in fields of repetitive elements such as a floor with hexagonal tiles or even a matrix of squares drawn on paper [*see fig. 7*]. If one stares at the matrix for a while, certain subsets of the squares will spontaneously organize themselves into simple figures. With voluntary effort one can attain fairly stable perceptions of rather complex figures. The most readily seen figures, however, tend to be simple, compact and symmetrical.

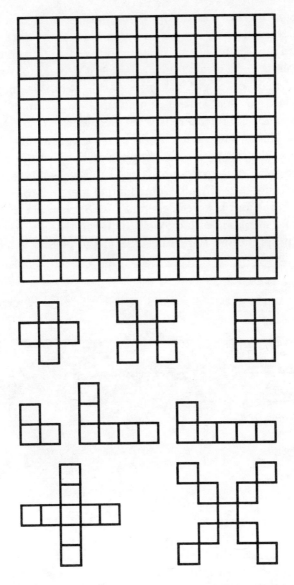

Figure 7–*Figural Groupings* occur when one stares at a matrix of squares. The simple figures organize themselves spontaneously and with effort more complex figures can be perceived. Some figures, however, are so complex that they are difficult to maintain.

Some of the most striking and amusing ambiguous figures are pictures (which may or may not involve figure-ground reversal) that can be seen as either of two familiar objects, for example a duck or a rabbit, a young girl or an old woman, and a man or a girl [*see figs. 8–10*]. What is meant by "familiar" in this context is that the visual inputs can be matched to some acquired or learned schemata of classes of objects. Just what such class schemata consist of—whether they are like composite photographs or like lists of properties —remains a matter of controversy. In any case the process of identification must involve some kind of matching between the visual input and a stored schema. If two schemata match the visual input about equally well, they compete for its perceptual interpretation; sometimes one of the objects is seen and

Figure 8–*Rabbit-Duck Figure* was used in 1900 by psychologist Joseph Jastrow as an example of rival-schemata ambiguity. When it is a rabbit, the face looks to the right; when it is a duck, the face looks to the left. It is difficult to see both duck and rabbit at the same time.

Figure 9–*Young Girl-Old Woman* was brought to the attention of psychologists by Edwin G. Boring in 1930. Created by cartoonist W. E. Hill, it was originally published in *Puck* in 1915 as "My Wife and My Mother-in-law." The young woman's chin is the old woman's nose.

sometimes the other. Therefore one reason ambiguity exists is that a single input can be matched to different schemata.

In certain ambiguous figures we can clearly see the nature of the positive feedback loop that accounts for the "locking in," or stabilization, of one or another aspect of the figure at any given time. For example, if in the young girl–old woman figure a certain line is tentatively identified as a nose, then a line below it must be the mouth and the shapes above must be the eyes. These partial identifications mutually support one another to form a stable perception of an old woman. If, however, the line we started with is seen as a chin instead of as a nose, then the perception formed is that of a young woman. The identification of wholes and of parts will

Figure 10– *Man-Girl Figures* are part of a series of progressively modified drawings devised by Gerald Fisher in 1967. He found that the last drawing in the top row has equal probability of being seen as a man or as a girl. Perception of middle pictures can be biased toward the man by viewing series in sequence beginning from top left and can be biased toward the girl by starting from bottom right.

likewise be reciprocally supportive, contributing further to the locking-in process.

Why one aspect of an ambiguous figure, once it is locked in, should ever give way to the other is a fundamental question. Indeed, a person can look for quite a long time at an ambiguous figure and see only one aspect of it. Robert Leeper of the University of Oregon showed that if a subject was first exposed to a version of the figure that was biased in favor of one of the interpretations, he would almost always see only that aspect in the ambiguous version. Not until the other aspect was pointed out would the figure spontaneously alternate. It is only after the input has made contact with both schemata that they become competitive. Making the initial contact and the associated organization must entail a type of learning.

Ambiguities of depth characterize a large class of multistable figures, of which the cube [*see fig. 11*] is the most familiar. In 1832 a Swiss geologist, Louis Albert Necker, pointed out that a drawing of a transparent rhomboid crystal could be seen in either of two different ways, that the viewer often

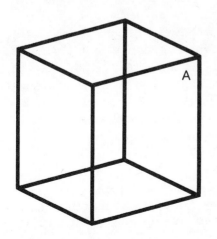

Figure 11–*Necker Cube,* a classic example of perspective reversal, is named after Louis Albert Necker, who in 1832 reported that line drawings of crystals appeared to reverse in depth spontaneously. Corner *A* alternates from front to back when gazed at steadily.

experiences "a sudden and involuntary change in the apparent position of a crystal or solid represented by an engraved figure." Necker concluded that the aspect seen depends entirely on the point of fixation, "the point of distinct vision" being perceived as the closer. Although the fixation point is indeed important, it has been shown that depth reversal will readily occur without eye movement.

If we want to understand how depth relationships can be multistable, we must first consider the more general question of how the perceptual system can derive a three-dimensional representation from a two-dimensional drawing. A straight line in the outside world casts a straight line on the retina. A given straight line on the retina, however, could be the image of any one of an infinite number of external lines, and not necessarily straight lines, that lie in a common plane with one another and the eye. The image on a single retina is always two-dimensional, exactly as a photograph is. We should not be surprised, therefore, that depth is sometimes ambiguous; it is far more remarkable that the perceptual system is able to select a particular orientation for a line segment (or at worst to vacillate between two or three orientations) out of the infinite number of legitimate possibilities that exist.

On what basis does the system perform this feat? According to the Gestalt psychologists the answer is to be found in a principle of *Prägnanz:* one perceives the "best" figure that is consistent with a given image. For most practical purposes "best" may be taken to mean "simplest." The advantage of this interpretation is that it is easier to find objective standards for complexity than for such qualities as being "best." One observes a particular configuration of lines on paper, such as the Necker cube, and assigns a three-dimensional orientation to the lines such that the whole becomes a cube (although an infinite number of noncubical forms could project the same form) because a cube is the simplest of the possibilities. In a cube the lines (edges) are all the same length; they take only three directions, and the angles they form are

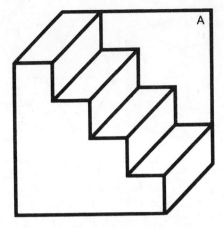

Figure 12–*Schroder Stairs* line drawing is another classic example of perspective reversal. Corner *A* is part of the rear wall when the staircase goes up the left; when reversal occurs, corner *A* becomes part of the front wall and the bottom of the stairway is seen.

all equal and right angles. No other interpretation of the figure, including the two-dimensional aspect itself, is as simple and regular. In cases of reversible perspective two maximally simple tridimensional constructions are permissible, each being symmetrical with the other in depth.

If this reasoning is correct, simple projections of a given solid should be perceived as being flat more often than complex projections of the same solid. Julian Hochberg and his colleagues at Cornell University studied various two-dimensional projections of a cube and other regular solids [*see fig. 13*]. Relatively complex projections are nearly always perceived in depth. A figure such as a regular hexagon divided into equilateral triangles, which is simple and regular in two dimensions, stays two-dimensional because seeing it as a cube does not make it any simpler. Intermediate figures become tristable; they are sometimes seen as being flat and sometimes as being one or another aspect of a cube. The measure of complexity devised by Hochberg and Virginia Brooks involved the number of continuous lines in the figure, the number of interior angles and the number of different angles. This measure predicted with considerable accuracy the pro-

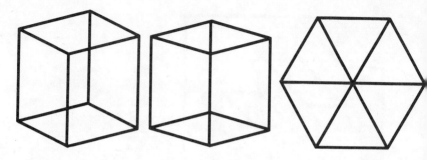

Figure 13–*Projections of a Cube* onto a two-dimensional surface are nearly always seen in depth when they resemble the Necker cube (left). As the projection becomes simpler and more regular it is more likely to be seen as a flat figure, such as a hexagon (right).

portion of the time that a figure was seen in depth rather than as being flat.

I have been emphasizing the importance of simplicity, but it is obvious that familiarity also plays an important role in instances of ambiguous depth. The two factors are hard to disentangle. Simple structures are experienced with great frequency, particularly in man-made environments. As Alvin G. Goldstein of the University of Missouri has shown by experiment, within limits a nonsense shape is judged to be simpler the more often it is experienced. In my view familiarity and simplicity become functionally equivalent in the perceptual system when a given input corresponds closely to a schema that is already well established by experience and can therefore be encoded or described (in the language of the nervous system) most simply in terms of that schema.

Depth reversal does not occur only with two-dimensional pictures. As the Austrian physicist and philosopher Ernst Mach pointed out, the perspective of many real objects will reverse when the object is viewed steadily with one eye. A transparent glass half-filled with water is a particularly

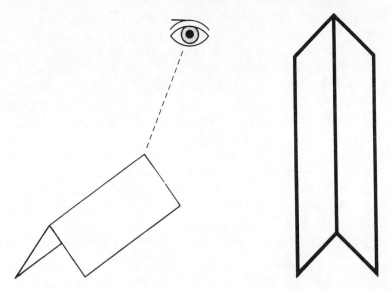

Figure 14–*Depth Reversal of a Real Object* can occur when it is viewed from above with one eye, an effect discovered by Ernest Mach. When a folded card is viewed from above and the front, it will appear to stand on end like an open book when it reverses. The same kind of depth reversal occurs with a simple line drawing of a folded card (above right).

dramatic example, but it requires considerable effort to achieve the reversal and the stability of the reversal is precarious. Mach discovered an easier reversal that is actually more instructive. Take a white card or a small piece of stiff paper and fold it once along its longitudinal axis [*see fig. 14*]. Place the folded card or paper in front of you on a table so that it makes a rooflike structure. Close one eye and view the card steadily for a while from directly above. It will reverse (or you can make it reverse) so that it appears as if the fold is at the bottom instead of the top. Now view the card with one eye from above at about a 45-degree angle so that the front of the folded card can be seen. After a few seconds the card will reverse and stand up on end like an open book with the inside toward you. If the card is assymmetrically illuminated and is seen in correct perspective, it will appear to be more or less white all over, as it is in reality, in spite of the fact that the illuminated plane reflects more light than the shadowed one. When the reversal occurs, the shadowed plane looks gray instead of white and the illuminated plane may appear luminous. In the perspective reversal the perceptual mechanism that preserves the constancy of reflectance is fooled; in order to maintain the relation between light source and the surfaces the perceptual system makes corrections that are erroneous because they are based on incorrect information.

Another remarkable phenomenon involving the folded card seems to have escaped Mach's notice. Recently Murray Eden of the Massachusetts Institute of Technology found that if after you make the folded card reverse you move your head slowly from side to side, the card will appear to rock back and forth quite as convincingly as if it were physically in motion. The explanation, very roughly, is that the mechanism that makes allowance for head movements, so that still objects appear still even though the head moves, is operating properly but on erroneous premises when the perspective is reversed. The perceived rocking of the card is exactly what would have to happen objectively if the card were really reversed to account for the sequence of retinal images accompanying head movement. What is remarkable about this is not that the mechanism can be wrong but rather that it can function so efficiently as a "lightning calculator" of complex problems in projective geometry and compensate so completely to maintain the perceived orientation. It seems to me that this capacity is a good argument for the existence of some kind of working model of three-dimensional space within the nervous system that solves problems of this type by analogue operations. Indeed, the basic concept of *Prägnanz*, of a system that finds its way to stable states that are simple by tri-dimensional criteria, is difficult to explain without also postulating a neural analogue model of three-dimensional space. We have no good theory at present of the nature of the neural organization that might subserve such a model.

A few years ago I stumbled on a principle of ambiguity that is different from any we have been considering. While planning an experiment on perceptual grouping I drew a number of equilateral triangles. After looking at them for a time I noticed that they kept changing in their orientation, sometimes pointing one way, sometimes another and sometimes a third way [*see fig. 15*]. The basis for this tristable ambiguity seems to be that the perceptual system can represent symmetry about only one axis at a time, even though an equilateral triangle is objectively symmetrical about three axes. In other words, an equilateral triangle is always perceived as being merely an isosceles triangle in some particular orientation. Compare any two sides or any two angles of an equilateral triangle and you will find that the triangle immediately points in the direction around which the sides and angles are symmetrical. When a group of equilateral triangles points upward, the triangles cease to fluctuate; the perceptual system strongly prefers the vertical axis of symmetry. Indeed, any perceived axis of symmetry seems to have the character of a locally rotated vertical.

When scalene triangles (triangles with three unequal sides) are grouped together with their corresponding sides parallel, they also appear to fluctuate in orientation after a brief inspection [*see fig. 15*]. This is at first puzzling since they have no axes of symmetry at all. The answer to the puzzle involves the third dimension: When the triangles are seen to point in a given direction, they simultaneously go into depth in such a way that they look like isosceles triangles seen at an angle. Perspective reversal doubles the possibilities, so that there are six ways the scalene triangles can be seen as isosceles. The same triangles may also be seen as right triangles in depth, with the obtuse angles most easily becoming the right angles.

Figure 15–*Equilateral Triangles* appear in one of three orientations depending on the dominant axis of symmetry (left). Usually all point in the same direction at one time, although the direction can change spontaneously. The scalene triangles (middle) fluctuate in orientation even though they are asymmetrical because they can also appear as isosceles or right triangles that point down or up. The same shape can be seen as either diamonds or tilted squares (right) depending on the orientation of the local reference system.

These observations begin to make sense if we suppose the perceptual system employs something quite like a Cartesian coordinate system to locate and describe things in space. (To call the system Cartesian is really putting the issue backward, since Descartes clearly took the primary perceptual directions of up-down, left-right and front-back as his reference axes.) The multistable states of triangles thus appear to involve simple relations between the figure and the reference system. The reference system may be tilted or rotated locally by the perceptual system and produce the apparent depth or orientation of the triangles.

In the same way we can explain how the same shape can appear to be so different when it is seen as a square or as a diamond. The square is perceived as having horizontal and vertical axes along its sides; the diamond is perceived as being symmetrical about a vertical axis running through opposite corners. Yet in certain kinds of grouping the perceptual axes can be locally rotated and the diamond can look like a tilted square [*see fig. 15*].

It should be evident by now that some principle of *Prägnanz*, or minimum complexity, runs as a common thread through most of the cases. It seems likely that the perceptual machinery is a teleogical system that is "motivated" to represent the outside world as economically as possible, within the constraints of the input received and the limitations of its encoding capabilities.

A good reason for invoking the concept of multistability to characterize figural ambiguity is that we know a great deal about multistable physical and electronic systems and may hope to apply some of this knowledge to the perceptual processes. The multistable behavior of the perceptual system displays two notable characteristics. The first is that at any one moment only one aspect of the ambiguous figure can be seen; mixtures or intermediate states occur fleetingly if at all. The second is that the different percepts alternate periodically. What accounts for this spontaneous alternation? Once the perceptual system locks into one aspect of the figure, why does it not remain in that state? An analogous physical system is a trapdoor that is stable only when it is either open or closed [*see fig. 16*].

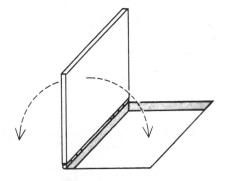

Figure 16–*Physical System* that exhibits a simple form of multistability is a trapdoor that is stable only when it is either open or shut.

As Necker pointed out, changing the point of visual fixation may cause perspective to reverse. In the instances where the input is being matched against more than one schema visual fixation on a feature that is more critical to one representation than the other may lock perception into only one aspect of the ambiguous figure. Since the percepts can alternate without a change in the point of fixation, however, some additional explanation is needed. The most likely is that the alternative aspects of the figure are represented by activity in different neural structures, and that when one such structure becomes "fatigued," or satiated or adapted, it gives way to another that is fresher and more excitable. Several investigators have noted that a reversing figure alternates more rapidly the longer it is looked at, presumably because both alternative neural structures build up some kind of fatigue. In some respects the neural structures behave like a multistable electronic circuit. A common example of multistability in electronic circuitry is the multivibrator flip-flop circuit, which can incorporate either vacuum tubes or transistors. In the vacuum tube version [*see fig. 17*] when one tube is

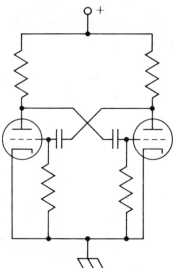

Figure 17–*Multivibrator Circuit* spontaneously alternates between *two* states. When one vacuum tube is conducting, the other is inhibited. A charge leaking from the coupling capacitor eventually starts the inhibited tube conducting. The positive feedback loop quickly makes it fully conducting and cuts off conduction in the first tube. The entire process is repeated in reverse, and the circuit flops from one state to the other.

conducting a current, the other tube is prevented from conducting by the low voltage on its grid. The plates and the grids of the two tubes are cross-coupled through capacitors, and one tube continues to conduct until the charge leaks from the coupling capacitor sufficiently for the other tube to start conducting. Once this tube begins to conduct, the positive feedback loop quickly makes it fully conducting and the other tube is cut off and becomes nonconducting. The process reverses and the system flip-flops between one state and the other.

What is "fatigued" in the multivibrator is the suppressive linkage. In other words, the inhibition of the nonconducting tube slowly weakens until it is no longer strong enough to prevent conduction. The possibility of an analogous neural process, in which the inhibition of the alternative neural structure progressively weakens, is worth considering.

Brain lesions may affect the perception of ambiguous figures. The finding most generally reported is that in people who have suffered brain damage the rate of alternation is lower, more or less independently of the locus of the lesion. On the other hand, a study of a group of brain-damaged war veterans conducted by Leonard Cohen at New York University indicated that damage to both frontal lobes increases the rate of alternation of a reversible figure, whereas damage to only one frontal lobe decreases the rate. The theoretical implications of these neurological findings are quite obscure and will doubtless remain so until we have some fundamental picture of the way the nervous system represents form and space.

You might try for yourself some of the illusions and experiments described in that article, particularly the one with the folded card (Mach). When you "see" that card standing upright and waving its head at you, you may be given pause for a moment about the evidence of your senses. And the evidence of your senses, as we've been suggesting, is a good thing to question once in a while.

For our writing assignment, however, we turn to an even more obvious experience of "multistability." On the cover of this book is an ink blot, one of those strange shapes calculated to exercise our visual imagination. Look at it, find a meaning in it. You may discover that if you look away from it and then look back again, you find new ways of seeing you had not experienced before.

Directions for Essay 2

Look carefully at the ink blot for several minutes. What do you see there? Write out your interpretation so that your reader can see what you see.

(Among the interpretations others have made of this ink blot are: two statues, two birds pecking food, a flower, a butterfly, two pelicans facing each other.)

Now force yourself to make a different interpretation —a different "reading" of these shapes. Write out your new interpretation as before.

Of the several interpretations now before you—yours and those of other observers—which one do you think is the best one? As you answer that question, what do you mean by "best"?

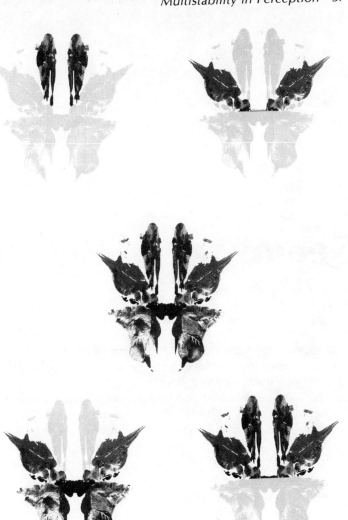

Figure 18–These are some of the things different people have reported seeing in the ink blot cover of this book. Did you see them? Looking back at the original ink blot, do you see them now? Have you perhaps been taught by other people what to see?

"I see," said the blind man, but he really didn't see at all.

Chapter
3
Seeing
Without Eyes

We have observed that to "see" something involves a lot more than a visual act and a simple translation of this act into words. The process is complicated. You have to decide on such things as a point of view, a purpose, an audience. You have to make a number of choices, both in the scene before your eyes and in the words you employ to your reader. In a very real sense, when you look at something and talk about it, you are making it. You create the world before you by the choices you commit yourself to. From hour to hour during any day of your life, you live in a world of frivolity or solemnity, variety or monotony, depending on how you choose to "look" at it. It is this aspect of looking as interpretation that is important to the writer, rather than of looking as a mere response of the visual nerves. In fact, the use of the words seeing, observing, examining, and so on to refer to mental acts of interpreting is very common in our language: for example, *look* at the first verb in this paragraph.

It is the choice, then, of the means of interpretation that creates the world we "see"—not simply the retinas of our eyes.

This was obviously true in the ambiguous pictures and the ink blot of chapter 2; it is in some sense true of all perception.

We confront the world, then, with certain limitations. We have been schooled to see only in certain ways; we have learned to select and edit experience quite unconsciously, to limit our vision. (It is absolutely necessary, of course, for us to do this.) More than that, our nervous system itself, as we have said, is an editing process that selects for us, whether we like it or not, what we think we "see."

In this chapter, we face that fact about the prejudgment or preselection of experience from another direction. Our very dependence on our eyes, in preference to other sense organs, means that we take in the world as a world of light and shadow. We are relatively insensitive to other ways of "seeing" experience—as smell, for instance, like a dog, or as sound, like a bat. This truth about man's special orientation becomes poignantly real for people who have lost their eyesight. In time, blind people learn to appreciate a world of great complexity and detail, without any eyes at all. That is the point of the two passages that follow. The first is by two experts on blindness (one of whom is blind), and it tells something of the curious way in which the world most of us think we live in is defined by the limited point of view of eyesight.

Sight and Light

HECTOR CHEVIGNY *and*
SYDELL BRAVERMAN

From the entrance of an apartment building fronting on a small city square, a man emerges holding a dog

From *The Adjustment of the Blind*, copyright 1950, by Hector Chevigny and Sydell Braverman. Reprinted by permission of Yale University Press.

on a leash. It is a male, a small bull terrier with a broad, flat nose and a quizzical expression. Whether the dog's expression is quizzical to another dog is problematic; the dog's face conveys that impression with certainty only to the man. Man and dog are relieved to be outdoors. It is a lovely day, chilly but sunny. The skies are blue and clear. The old buildings that front the square look a little less dingy than usual; the deposit of city grime and soot on them looks almost beautiful. Upon the nature of the difference between beauty and ugliness, however, neither man nor dog pauses to think.

They cross to the little park in the center of the square. A small patch of grass lies there; a few flowers in beds are growing bravely; the trees are budding. The dog pulls his master along from object to upright object, smelling each of them carefully. He inspects the lampposts, the trees, the fire hydrants. It is quite evident that he enjoys doing this. After a while he will tire of it and lie down, but for the time being he acts as if he had been longing, for several hours, to do some smelling and now cannot cover the range of objects fast enough. . . .

The man is also busily employing his sensorial apparatus. He looks. He stands and stares or glances about as he follows the dog. The colors intrigue him. He looks at the new green paint on the benches, at the grass, at the budding trees, at what Wilde termed "that little tent of blue which prisoners call the sky." He has been reading all morning and, in addition to whatever emotional stimulus he gets from the awareness of intake of light, there is pleasure in stretching the complex muscles of his eyes. There is always pleasure in sheer functioning under optimal conditions and he drinks in this pleasure now. Meanwhile, on a more or less subconscious plane of operation, his sight also functions to guide him as he walks. He watches the traffic, he notes the curbs and the obstructions about him. Data furnished by sound, smell, and touch, in addition to those given by sight, he heeds little. They seem not merely of subsidiary importance but no importance whatever as a contribution to his knowledge of where he is.

His most conscious preoccupation is with the beauty of the scene. Color and degrees of difference in shade certainly create some of this for him. It is useless to enter into the question of whether beauty, or ugliness either, has objective reality; subjective reality they both have. The man is a heliotropic creature. He loves light. Light is associated with well-being, the dark with ill-being. He fears the dark, or at least he fears the need for movement in it. He feels his sight cannot avail him there, but that is not the only reason he distrusts it. He envisions Heaven as filled with light of an immense, perpetual clarity. Dante and Milton have given expression to this belief. Hell is black and gruesome, lighted by cruel fires that only accentuate the dark.

Mythology carries much evidence of symbolism between eye and sun. Horus, god of the sun, had as his symbol the human eye. In the Vedas the sun is called "the eye of the world." Santa Lucia (Holy Light) is the patron saint of eye diseases; she had her martyrdom on the shortest day of the year. The birth of sungods in mythology usually has been associated with the winter solstice.

It is necessary for his well-being that man receive a certain amount of light. So intense is his tropism for light that it is highly probable this has conditioned much of his phylogenetic and cultural development. He has always had a wish to extend himself upward, toward the skies. Maybe this is a wish for God, maybe for the sun; take your choice according to your own lights—and this figure of speech indicates part of our identification of truth with light.

The man, because his sight is the most immediate perceptor of light he has, thinks it is the only receptor of it. His entire organism, however, knows when he has been deprived of light for any length of time. This is more than a matter of feeling mere warmth. His skin is sensitive to it, undergoing change or exposure or removal from it, and reacts in fact to rays the eye cannot perceive. The man's innermost being knows when it is day and when it is night. It is a fable that the blind know the difference between night and day only by the custom by which they live. A vast pulse beat goes through all nature. Vitality rises and falls almost like the tides. Man's stamina is at its lowest in the small hours of morning and his fevers highest at night. The man's certainty that only his eye appreciates light is one of the first overestimations of the role his sight plays in the pattern of his living.

The dog is not so photocentric a creature. In his wild state he is most active at night. His sense of sight, by comparison with man's, is inferior. He is not very good at distinguishing colors. Indeed, whether he can tell the difference among some colors, including red and green, is questionable. It is not true that the Seeing-Eye dog can note the change in traffic lights. But his senses of hearing and smell are very acute. His sense of hearing has been estimated to be sixteen times greater than man's and his olfactory sense so much more acute that calculation of the difference is almost impossible.

The man's superiority over the dog lies in the senses of sight and kinesthesia. Whether the latter in man is actually more acute than it is in the dog is open to question, but it is certainly trained to greater fineness. The man's habit of walking erect keeps him ever on the alert for emergencies. The dog, placed on four legs, has an easier time of it. The man must make finer distinctions in the matter of space and depth and estimate distances more accurately. His binocular vision aids in appreciating depth and perspective. The images from those two cameras, the eyes, fuse and amalgamate by the interlocked distribution system of sight in the brain, to create the impression of one image which, however, has perspective by virtue of the two superimposed images. Man thus adds a further element through his sight to his esthetic system, and in this the distinction in artfulness is made between the photograph and the work of the artist.

All these matters are almost invariably under the control of the involuntary system. The man, however, believes that his conscious will directs them through his eyes. He thinks his sight guards against his falling or stumbling. It seems to be the case with most people that their involuntary attention does assign greater validity to the visual than to the auditory or kinesthetic. Our man, as he goes about, is greatly aided by his hearing in orienting himself, but to the data from hearing he pays little conscious attention. He therefore finds it hard to understand how a man without sight does not stumble more frequently and easily than he does.

The dog's ability to smell is, in the opinion of some observers, and at least under undomestic circumstances, the sense by which he is most quickly made aware of events and objects of interest to him at a distance. It would seem that what the wind carries he can perceive by smell some time before even his keen hearing can catch and classify the information. Both dog and man, then, use the sense which affords each of them the greatest perception of things at a distance as the channel on which they also depend most for stimulation enjoyed for its own sake.

The reception of a stimulus by the retina depends, of course, upon the transmittal to it of light waves. Recent research on the nature of olfaction seems to indicate that this hitherto little understood process also depends upon the reception of radiation of waves, of extremely high frequency, carried by gases. But this is of only minor interest. An esthetic cannot be reasoned out for the dog, even knowing the nature of the sensory process by which he seems to enjoy himself the most, because no one knows what differences, in either kind or degree, he detects in the substances he smells. We do not know, for the most part, what he finds repugnant and what he does not. In the man's case, however, some basis for the knotty problem of esthetics on which philosophers have written tons of books may be worked out in oversimplified form. Colors give pleasure because they are parts of light, components of the spectrum, and are therefore attached to the main body of the stimulating force, namely, light. The ugly is essentially the dark thing, that which is somber, unclear. The dichotomy between good and evil is indicated in the distinction between light and shade. In the well-ordered pattern comprising both, with gradations of color in each, man can see that balance and control between the good and the bad which he seeks perpetually in all living. The feelings of goodness constituted by light he carries over to ideas having nothing to do with seeing. "Light" is an adjective which, as opposed to heavy, indicates that which is capable of rising toward the sky. And in the combination of the two words "heavy" and "dark" the connotation of the ominous, the evil, is carried.

Man consistently makes one mistake in his preoccupation with light. Regarding it as a positive quality, he regards absence of light also as a positive quality, calling it "the dark" and assuming that it actually can be seen. One of the most difficult of all ideas for him to grasp emotionally is that when he "sees" dark he is not seeing it at all but is merely reacting to the absence of light—in other words, that he sees nothing.

One of the remarkable facts connected with this entire situation is that the pain man believes must be caused by the absence of sight he does not also feel to be caused by the absence of hearing. . . .

The power to conceive mentally is so thoroughly equated with visual terms that the language has only the word "imagination" to express it. The word expresses only the idea of picture. If one wishes to speak of conception in terms of touch or hearing, he has to invent phrases such as "auditory imagination" and "tactual imagination." When the art of educating the blind child began to develop, it was found there were no words by which to convey its concepts. These contradictory phrases had to be resorted to. When the phonograph was invented it was found that the language had no word to convey the idea of a captured sound impression in the sense that the words "picture" and "image" indicate a caught sight impression. The inadequate word "record" was selected.

To express comprehension one uses words almost exclusively related to seeing and visualization; he "sees the point," he "views the situation," he "takes a look" or "glances at the evidence." Much less frequently are comprehensive words based on other senses: we do "grasp a problem."

When the evidence of the senses concerning reality conflicts, many will ignore the grossest evidence in favor of what their sight tells them. Witkin and his associates at Brooklyn College showed by carefully controlled experiments that some individuals when sitting in a chair tilted as much as thirty degrees will stubbornly deny the evidence of their sense of balance and believe they are sitting upright because the experimental chamber is designed to convey this visual impression. Witkin also showed that in conflicts between sight and hearing over the origin of sources of sound a surprisingly large number will trust their sight rather than their hearing. An unexplained result of these experiments is that women tend more than men to "believe what they see."

People found it so difficult to believe that the blind child could be educated for the reason that they had to imagine a condition of mind in which, to them, there could be no imagination. Because they could not imagine how understanding in the blind child could develop without imagination, there apparently had to be a "void" in the mind of the blind. When the educability of the blind was demonstrated, theories whereby the other senses transmitted visual impressions were invented to account for it.

Dreams show the extent to which the exercise of the understanding revolves around the visual and the imaginative. Impressions usually interpreted in terms other than sight and even abstractions reduce to pictures. Abstractions, in the dream, never occur as such but condense into pictures, sometimes grotesquely but always possible of reinterpretation in the waking state back to the abstract. A lad dreamed of the abstraction "parents" and saw a composite figure of his father and mother. How sound often translates in the dream into imagery is illustrated by the case of the girl who dreamed of a firecracker going off but instead of hearing the explosion saw the giant word "Bang!" on a great billboard.

Sight comes later than the use of his other senses in the growth of the child. But once it arrives the child begins using it to verify reality as he has learned of it through touch, hearing, and his other senses. It soon seems to assume generalship over the sensorium. The growth of the mental faculties seems to follow this same patterning of events, visualization becoming the focal point for almost all that the adult conceives of as reality. Grasp of reality, or "understanding," becomes identical with visualization. And visualization is shaped by the ability to see. The three become equated, understanding with visualization with sight. Cutting out the middle element, understanding becomes equated with sight.

This equation has bound man to the finite and the material. Because of it he fashioned his very gods after his own image and the images of other creatures he knew. Only the exercise of his highest reason could release him from the equation and show him that what he had conceived of as the unknown was not what he had never seen but that which could not be envisioned. Then, at lengthy and painful last, man knew that what is godlike is that which is beyond the capability of sight ever to capture. . . .

The Darkness Concept

The notion that under blindness there is a constant conscious awareness of absence of light—and therefore an awareness of darkness—has not received much attention from the psychologists, with the exception of Cutsforth. One must begin to examine, with very conscious attention indeed, the language one uses, to note how frequent is reference to the darkness concept. Literature is so deeply imbued with it that it is questionable if the concept can ever be eradicated. There is hardly a book on any phase of the blind problem which is not titled with some variant of the phrase "out of the dark." The senior author's earlier work on blindness inveighed against the concept at some length, yet not only was the review of the book in one of the major New York papers titled "Out of the Darkness" but its text referred twice to "the dark world of the blind."

In speaking of hope in connection with the blind, the word light is used to indicate it. The nation's famous agency is dubbed the Lighthouse. Over the door of the New York Guild for the Jewish Blind appears this sentence: "For all who, in a world of untold beauty, are consigned to darkness, here is light."

Such phrases, except insofar as they tend to reinforce the notion that the blind live in a state of perpetual gloom and melancholy, would probably be little more than euphemistic, did they not do further mischief in suggesting, and so constantly, the void concept. In the effort to imagine what blindness must be like, virtually everyone has, no doubt, at one time or another, shut his eyes. Is it not odd that after having noted the feeling of darkness, those who tried this little experiment did not also note that the feeling of being in the dark passes, after a brief time, to be replaced by the photisms of the imagination? Many blind people do "see" some pervasive color element; usually it is a natural gray but in some it is a constant or intermittent display of what they term "fireworks," which is doubtless due to pathology in the retina. Except for this, what the blind "see" consists of the same photisms of the imagination known to the sighted. "The conclusion that the blind must live in a world of darkness," says Cutsforth,

has been derived through faulty reasoning from Newtonian Physics . . . and if blackness, or darkness, is the opposite of light, then the blind live in a world of complete darkness. The implication is that the blind who so desperately desire to see are confronted, by their inability, with a world of experiential darkness filled with all the horrors of gloom, fear, loneliness, and whatever else the timorous seeing experience in the dark. This is as untrue psychologically as it is physically. . . .

The next passage is from an autobiography written by a young man who, in the spring of 1941, was blinded by a gunshot wound while he was still a college undergraduate. Here he tells of some of his early attempts to become adjusted to "this foreign setting" after he had begun to recover from his wound and had to face the fact of his blindness.

Cast Off the Darkness
PETER PUTNAM

My intellectual acceptance of the obvious fact went no further than the statement "I am blind," and the statement had little meaning because it had little application. . . . I was like a traveler who, having missed his ship in some remote port of call, finds that there will not be another one for several weeks or months. There was nothing to do but wait, and while I waited I might as well make myself at home in this foreign setting.

My first and most obvious problem was simply that of finding my way around. In my bedroom, I depended on my hands for orientation. To get to the bathroom, I would feel my way along the length of my bed, take one free-standing step to grope for the corner of the bureau with my left hand, and then pivot around it to reach for the door with my right. Somewhat to my surprise, the stairs were simple. I had to approach them warily, but once I had located the top step, the equal spacing of the treads and the touch of the banister under my hand made descent easy. In the more complicated furniture arrangement of the living room, I used my legs as well as my hands for orientation. The contact of my calves with the seat of a chair was a clue to the direction of the doorway, or my knee brushing the edge of the coffee table made clear the position of the sofa. My most consistent failure was a tendency to overestimate distance. Every room in the house seemed to have shrunk to two-thirds of its former size, and until I had learned to slow and shorten my stride, I was continually barging into things.

I could always ask my family for guidance, but this, too, had its difficulties. It was hard to make verbal instructions precise, and we were amazed at how often we confused left and right when facing each other. On the other hand, to be grabbed by the arms and pushed or pulled in the desired direction was both clumsy and annoying. It was much easier to put my hand on my guide's shoulder and to follow along a little behind and to one side.

Getting around the house was far more awkward than walking outdoors. I recall the first evening my mother and I stepped outside. I kept my hand on her shoulder down the driveway, but after we had turned into the road I let go, and held a parallel course by the sound of her footsteps. There were no distances to gauge and no furniture to bump into, so that I could walk without hesitating and without holding my hands a little in front of me. I was carrying a cane for balance, and as I swung it along beside me, I felt positively jaunty.

There was another reason for my jauntiness that evening, for that was the first time I had got myself fully dressed. After the weeks in pajamas, my clothes seemed coarse and heavy, but I felt stronger and more confident with each item I put on. I can still remember in the minutest detail everything I wore that evening. It was terribly important to me to know exactly how I looked, and this longing for familiarity was accompanied by an exaggerated fastidiousness. The notion that my pants might be baggy, my shoes unshined, or my tie spotted was somehow humiliating, and I took the most elaborate precautions with my appearance. . . .

I tried to discipline my memory and developed a fanatical zeal for neatness, but time and again I would misplace my tie clasp or belt or shoe polish. As I groped through drawers or under the bed, my exasperation mounted steadily, and whenever I was forced to call for help, I was inwardly boiling.

My irritability often turned against others, when their help seemed clumsy or misguided. For example, when I asked where I had put my tie clasp, I meant just that. I wanted to be directed to it, to feel it out myself, and to profit from my mistake. It annoyed me to have it placed in my hand instead. There was some logic in my reasoning, but my irritability was out of all proportion to the occasion, and I cursed myself afterward.

The true source of my impatience with others was my impatience with myself. My efforts to acquire some tolerance for my own blindness were exhausting. I remember the herculean struggles of my first attempt to change my typewriter ribbon. It took forever, and I came to hate the cobweb silken softness of the ribbon, which oozed its ink into my trembling fingers and bent and curled and twisted, but would not slip into the hair-thin grooves of the ribbon guides and carrier. Repeatedly I leaned back in my chair to rest, and two or three times I rose, washed the ink from my sweating hands, and smoked an entire cigarette, thinking it out in my mind and trying to soothe the nervousness that made my hands shake and my heart pound. When it was over at last, I lay down on my bed to listen to the whole of Beethoven's Seventh.

That summer my records were almost an emotional necessity. It was a rare day that I did not spend two or three hours listening to them. They were not simply a means of escape. Apart from the discipline required to memorize the arrangement of two hundred records, I was using them as therapy for my frustrations. Whenever I sensed the approach of one of those fits of nervous exhaustion I had first noticed in the hospital, I would lie down on my bed and listen to music until my balance was restored. This was a form of introspection, but it had the affirmative aim of action, for it helped me to pace myself to my limitations.

In one instance, blindness proved not to be a limitation. About a month after my first walk, I was coming downstairs into the hall when some instinct made me jerk back my head. Putting out my hand, I found that my involuntary movement had saved my forehead a nasty bump on the supporting column at the foot of the staircase.

In a flash, I realized what had happened. Only a few days before, my sister had read me an article in *Life* on a phenomenon called "facial vision." Facial vision, it explained, was a faculty developed by the blind for estimating the distance, direction, and approximate size of unseen obstacles from the barely audible echoes of incidental sounds reflecting from them. It is a sort of natural radar in which footsteps, voices, or even air currents play the part of sound impulses rebounding from opposing surfaces.

I was fascinated by my first experience of it and stood there for some time, moving my head back and forth beside the column. Each time I approached, there was a looming sensation, more like feeling than hearing. Later, I found that I could duplicate it by moving my hand toward my ear. I often practiced it sitting in a chair, and when I walked, either indoors or out, I would listen intently for the telltale contraction of echoes when I passed through a doorway or under a tree. I played with my discovery as one might play with a new toy.

As a matter of fact, I played with blindness on a number of levels throughout the summer. One of my most absorbing preoccupations was the exploration of it as a social handicap.

With the return of my brother Lo from prep school, my horizons widened. He brought friends to the house and drove me to the houses of other people. Together we took walks, attended the movies, and went to several parties. . . . Lo was not unsympathetic toward my blindness, but he did not seem to be fearful about it. Like me, he viewed it with objective curiosity, investigating its mysteries and experimenting with it in a way that my parents would have found impossible. Many of these experiments were aimless, but they will seem cruel only to those who have forgotten the invulnerability that is also called the indolence, the indifference, and the resilience of youth.

It was inevitably my brother with whom I felt most closely bound in this experimental attitude, but it is clearly illustrated by an incident during a visit from two college classmates, Gordy Bent and Bobby Harvey. They were sitting in my room one morning talking while I dressed, when I noticed an undercurrent of laughter in their conversation.

When I asked what was so funny, their laughter broke into the open.

"It didn't work," Gordy said. "We were trying to fool you."

"We switched your lifeline," Bobby explained, "to see if it wouldn't throw you off, but you've been wandering around for five minutes without making a single mistake."

My "lifeline" was a piece of string tied between my bedpost and the bathroom door. Originally I had used it only to make my way to the lavatory, but they had noticed that I now made frequent contacts with it for purposes of general orientation. Curious to see what would happen, they had transferred one end to another door.

A similar curiosity prompted all sorts of different experiments. While we were taking a walk that same day, Bobby had stopped me, turned me around a few times to confuse my sense of direction, and then asked me to point to where I thought the sun was. Guiding me down a flight of steps, Gordy ducked the shoulder I had my hand on after we had reached the bottom to fool me into taking another downward step. Later in the summer, my brother darted around on the beach to see whether I could follow the sound of his footsteps in the sand, and ran ahead of me, shouting instructions, while I tested my equilibrium on a precarious bicycle ride. There was no immediate purpose to be served by such experiments, but they were useful as explorations of the extent to which my blindness was or was not a handicap.

[In the next section, from an earlier book of Mr. Putnam's, he tells of returning to college for a football week end during the fall following the summer just described.]

The street was Prospect, the town was Princeton, and the excitement which surrounded and warmed me on all sides was that of a gala college football Saturday two hours before game time. . . . We turned off the walk to the right, and Dick's voice cut through my connections with the impersonal crowd and brought me instantly back into contact with my friends.

"Where are we now, Pete?" he asked.

"Easy," I said. "The University Cottage Club." I removed my hand from his shoulder, handed him my cane, and performed a low salaam. They all laughed.

"How'd you know?" Ann asked. "I didn't."

"The brick walk," I kicked my heel against its surface, "portends the 'Brick Shack.' "

"The 'Brick Shack'?"

"The name," I explained, "which the unlettered sometimes apply to the elegant pile before us." Ann laughed cheerfully at almost anything, so I pointed my cane and went on, very pleased with my own success. "Note the classic simplicity of the Georgian style and the geometric effect of the white marble quoins setting off the . . ."

From *Keep Your Head Up, Mr. Putnam!* by Peter Putnam. Copyright, 1952, by Peter Putnam. Reprinted by permission of Harper & Brothers.

"Cut it out!" Ben said. "I get enough of that stuff in Art 306."

"He's not really blind," Ann said. "He's faking."

"I'm dodging the draft," I said, pleased again. "Once I get a Seeing Eye dog to replace this cane, my disguise will be impenetrable."

"Slacker!" Dick said. "Look out, now! We're coming to the door."

Inside, the clamor of voices engulfed us. As we threaded our way through the standing crowd, there was a shout of "Hi, Pete!" from across the room. I smiled and shouted back, but I did not recognize the voice, and we were headed in the opposite direction.

"Let go of Dick," Ben said, "and give me your other hand."

I did as I was told, and he pulled me through.

"God, what a crush!" I said, "and, boy, how I love it!"

"Here we go," Ben said. "Down these steps."

"Where are you taking me? Don't lock me in the cellar. I want to stay with all the pretty girls."

"All the pretty girls are right behind you," Ann said.

"The alumni had a bar put in the basement this summer," Dick explained. "Wait'll you see it. It's very classy. We're meeting Sandy down there."

I followed Ben down the stairs. We turned left, walked a few paces, and turned again down a longer flight of stairs. At the bottom, we turned right, and I could tell by the sudden contractions of the echoes that we were going through a door. There were many people sitting in this new room, and as we walked, I twisted my body sideways with each rotation of Ben's shoulder to avoid the crowded tables and chairs. I was grateful to Ben for our swift sure passage across the room.

"Hey, group!" Ben called.

The answering shouts came, I guessed, from a table in front of us. I recognized the boys' voices, and I was introduced to two new girls.

"Here's a chair," Dick said, pushing it behind my knees so that I nearly fell into it.

"Easy does it!" I said and reached to my breast pocket for a cigarette. That was something I had gotten into the habit of doing as soon as I came into a new room. It furnished a protective screen of action, behind which I could take my bearings and listen to the relative position of people's voices without seeming to do so. Sandy Prentiss, one of the strange girls and Ben Williamson were on my left. Ann Wylie, Dick Sayer and Dave Compton were on my right. The rest, I decided, were too far away to matter, but I felt a renewed tingle of excitement at the thought that I was back among them.

"Here!" Sandy took my hand and put a drink in it. "Force a little bourbon down your throat."

"Thanks," I said. I took a long drink and settled back as Dick launched into an enthusiastic description of the new bar.

That was how it began, and it seemed like a very fine beginning. We finished our drinks and had another. We talked and laughed in shouts above the clatter of the room, and our conversation was all what we used to call "the old cheap chatter." Dave Compton insisted on taking me up to the bar to test the rail, and when I put my foot on it and called, "Look Ma, no hands," everybody laughed. Everybody laughed at everything. For a while, I rode with the crest of my exhilaration at being back, and the warmth of the whiskey, and the social distinction my blindness gave me, but, then, without any warning, the wave passed over my head and left me floating in its receding wake. I felt tired, removed, a little ashamed of the flush on my face, and, as the remembered sound of my own voice rang in my ears, I was suddenly convinced that my part in the cheap chatter had been really cheap. I had been subject to such emotional oscillations since my blindness and should have been able to guard against them, but Prospect, the club, the girls, the whiskey, and the old friends had been too much for me after the months of absence. I would have to slow down, and I was glad I had arranged to stay in the club instead of going to the game.

"Drink up, everybody!" Dave Compton called. "Let's get this show on the road. If we don't get upstairs and grab some lunch, we'll be late for the kickoff."

"You children toddle on ahead and get your roughage," Sandy said. "Pete and I are going to have another drink. We never eat on an empty stomach."

"Are you sure you wouldn't rather go to the game?" I asked. "You don't have to stay with me, you know. I'd be fine by myself."

"I'd rather hear it on the radio," Sandy said. "I'm too nearsighted to see anything anyway."

Dick was standing behind my chair.

"We could still get you a ticket if you'd rather go," he said.

"No, this is fine," I said. "I'm kind of tired. I'll meet you here afterward."

We lingered in the empty bar for a while after the others had gone, and then Sandy took me upstairs, through the deserted hall and out into the terrace court. A lone waiter was noisily piling plates and glasses upon a metal tray. The surface warmth of the sun on my face gave me the feeling of the brightness of the day. Sandy led me forward across the terrace to a comfortably cushioned cane sofa, and I sat down while he went back inside to get us each a plate from the buffet. The leatherette of the cushion was warm against my legs and back. Behind me, in the court, a trickle of water splashed in the little stone fountain where goldfish were sometimes kept in the spring. Ahead of me, down the slope of the hill, the muffled voice of the loudspeaker announced the pertinent statistics of each play, and the occasional roars of the crowd wavered up to me on the soft breath of the cool wind. A fly lit on the back of my hand, making a tiny spot of cold. Dreamily, I pondered this for a moment. Maybe the fly's body was itself cold, or, maybe, even in those few square millimeters of shadow, the absence of the sun was noticeable on the surface of my skin. I slapped and was pleased to feel it, for an instant, under my fingers at the moment of contact, and I remembered, then, that flies got sluggish and easy to kill in the fall. Sandy came out on the terrace behind me.

"I just killed my first fly in six months," I said.

"Good," Sandy said. "Glad to see you keeping yourself amused. Here's food."

He set down the plates on a coffee table in front of us. I was hungry, and I ate with concentration. There was some tomato aspic that kept falling off my fork, and I was glad there was nobody but Sandy there to see. I felt relaxed and secure there on the terrace, and I was ready to suggest that Sandy turn on the livingroom radio loud enough so that we could hear it without moving, but he spoke first.

"Dick tells me you're planning to get a Seeing Eye dog."

"That's right."

"Does that mean there's no more hope for your eyes?"

"I suppose there's always hope for a miracle," I said. "The bullet hardly touched my eyes at all, but the optic nerves are pretty well shot. I don't even have light perception. If there were anything left of the nerves, there should have been some sign of it long ago."

"That's tough."

"I'm lucky I didn't get killed."

Now you should be ready to try an experiment yourself—to "see" a world without using your eyes. This is an exercise in sense perception: hearing, smelling, touching, tasting. But it has a more ambitious purpose too. It suggests, of course, that the world we think we live in is simply the world we do in fact perceive and express, in whatever way we do perceive and express it. The world most of us live in, as Chevigny and Braverman remind us, is a world lit up, a photocentric existence in which our very notion of the way we think is told in metaphors of light. (We see the light at last.) To be blind seems to be one way of living, often quite satisfactorily, in another sort of world altogether, where metaphors of light are simply not appropriate. If all men were blind, the effect on language would be staggering.

Directions for Essay 3

Chose a particular place—the place of essay 1 or some other of your choice—and blindfold or close your eyes tightly for at least ten or fifteen minutes. Then write a description, as sensitive as you can make it, of what you "saw" under these circumstances, through your senses of touch, smell, taste, and hearing.

SEE (sī), v. Pa.t. SAW; pa.pple. SEEN. [Com.
Teut.str.vb.; OE.séon. derived from pre-Teut.
sequ-, of disputed relationship.] . . . 3. (fig.)
trans. *To perceive mentally; to apprehend
by thought (a truth, etc.), to recognize the
force of (a demonstration). Often with ref.
to metaphorical light or eyes. ME. . . . 4.
trans. With mixed literal and fig. sense: To
perceive by visual tokens. ME. b. To learn by
reading. late ME.*
THE SHORTER OXFORD ENGLISH DICTIONARY

Chapter

4

Learning

to See

The two well known passages in this section are by writers skilled at seeing. The first, by a scientist, offers a way of seeing a fish, a way of "reading" details to make classifications. And the second, by Mark Twain, offers an experience of reading-by-seeing the Mississippi River, an interpretation of details for a purpose.

In the first passage, a student of the nineteenth-century scientist Louis Agassiz tells how he was taught to see a fish. This sounds simple, but, as you will discover in his account, it took Nathaniel Shaler a long time to learn how Agassiz wanted him to see. The questions we will ask, which Shaler only partially answers in this passage, are these: Just how does one learn to *see* something, besides simply spending a long time at it? Just what was it Shaler was able to do with his fish, after he had learned to see it, that he hadn't been able to do before? We already know that seeing something is more than simply directing one's eyes on it for a period of time. Does Shaler offer any further hints as to what this "more" may be?

Seeing a Fish

NATHANIEL SOUTHGATE SHALER

At the time of my secession from the humanities, Agassiz was in Europe; he did not return, I think, until the autumn of 1859. I had, however, picked up several acquaintances among his pupils, learned what they were about, and gained some notion of his methods. After about a month he returned, and I had my first contact with the man who was to have the most influence on my life of any of the teachers to whom I am indebted. I shall never forget even the lesser incidents of this meeting, for this great master by his presence gave an importance to his surroundings, so that the room where you met him and the furniture stayed with the memory of him.

When I first met Louis Agassiz, he was still in the prime of his admirable manhood; though he was then fifty-two years old, and had passed his constructive period, he still had the look of a young man. His face was the most genial and engaging that I had ever seen, and his manner captivated me altogether. But as I had been among men who had a free swing, and for a year among people who seemed to me to be cold and super-rational, hungry as I doubtless was for human sympathy, Agassiz's welcome went to my heart—I was at once his captive. It has been my good chance to see many men of engaging presence and ways, but I have never known his equal. . . .

While Agassiz questioned me carefully as to what I had read and what I had seen, he seemed in this preliminary going

From *Autobiography of Nathaniel Southgate Shaler* (Boston: Houghton Mifflin Company, 1907). Reprinted by permission of the estate of Gabriella Shaler Webb.

over in no wise concerned to find what I knew about fossils, rocks, animals, and plants; he put aside the offerings of my scanty lore. This offended me a bit, as I recall, for the reason that I thought I knew, and for a self-taught lad really did know, a good deal about such matters, especially as to the habits of insects, particularly spiders. It seemed hard to be denied the chance to make my parade; but I afterward saw what this meant—that he did not intend to let me begin my tasks by posing as a naturalist. The beginning was indeed quite different, and, as will be seen, in a manner that quickly evaporated my conceit. It was made and continued in a way I will now recount.

Agassiz's laboratory was then in a rather small two-storied building, looking much like a square dwelling-house, which stood where the College Gymnasium now stands . . . Agassiz had recently moved into it from a shed on the marsh near Brighton bridge, the original tenants, the engineers, having come to riches in the shape of the brick structure now known as the Lawrence Building. In this primitive establishment Agassiz's laboratory, as distinguished from the store-rooms where the collections were crammed, occupied one room about thirty feet long and fifteen feet wide—what is now the west room on the lower floor of the edifice. In this place, already packed, I had assigned to me a small pine table with a rusty tin pan upon it. . . .

When I sat me down before my tin pan, Agassiz brought me a small fish, placing it before me with the rather stern requirement that I should study it, but should on no account talk to anyone concerning it, nor read anything relating to fishes, until I had his permission so to do. To my inquiry, "What shall I do?" he said in effect: "Find out what you can without damaging the specimen; when I think that you have done the work I will question you." In the course of an hour I thought I had compassed that fish; it was rather an unsavory object, giving forth the stench of old alcohol, then loathsome to me, though in time I came to like it. Many of the scales were loosened so that they fell off. It appeared to me to be a case for a summary report, which I was anxious to make and get on to the next stage of the business. But Agassiz, though always within call, concerned himself no further with me that day, nor the next, nor for a week. At first, this neglect was distressing; but I saw that it was a game, for he was, as I discerned rather than saw, covertly watching me. So I set my wits to work upon the thing, and in the course of a hundred hours or so thought I had done much—a hundred times as much as seemed possible at the start. I got interested in finding out how the scales went in series, their shape, the form and placement of the teeth, etc. Finally, I felt full of the subject, and probably expressed it in my bearing; as for words about it then, there were none from my master except his cheery "Good morning." At length, on the seventh day, came the question, "Well?" and my disgorge of learning to him as he sat on the edge of my table puffing his cigar. At the end of the hour's telling, he swung off and away, saying: "That is not right." Here I began to think that, after all, perhaps the rules for scanning Latin verse were not the worst infliction in the world. Moreover, it was clear that he was playing a game with me to find if I were capable of doing hard, continuous work without the support of a teacher, and this stimulated me to labor. I went at the task anew, discarded my first notes, and in another week of ten hours a day labor I had results which astonished myself and satisfied him. Still there was no trace of praise in words or manner. He signified that it would do by placing before me about a half a peck of bones, telling me to see what I could make of them, with no further directions to guide me. I soon found that they were the skeletons of half a dozen fishes of different species; the jaws told me so much at a first inspection. The task evidently was to fit the separate bones together in their proper order. Two months or more went to this task with no other help than an occasional looking over my grouping with the stereotyped remark: "That is not right." Finally, the task was done, and I was again set upon alcoholic specimens—this time a remarkable lot of specimens representing, perhaps, twenty species of the side-swimmers or Pleuronectidae.

I shall never forget the sense of power in dealing with things which I felt in beginning the more extended work on a group of animals. I had learned the art of comparing objects, which is the basis of the naturalist's work. At this stage I was allowed to read, and to discuss my work with others about me. I did both eagerly, and acquired a considerable knowledge of the literature of ichthyology, becoming especially interested in the system of classification, then most imperfect. I tried to follow Agassiz's scheme of division into the order of ctenoids and ganoids, with the result that I found one of my species of side-swimmers had cycloid scales on one side and ctenoid on the other. This not only shocked my sense of the value of classification in a way that permitted of no full recovery of my original respect for the process, but for a time shook my confidence in my master's knowledge. At the same time I had a malicious pleasure in exhibiting my "find" to him, expecting to repay in part the humiliation which he had evidently tried to inflict on my conceit. To my question as to how the nondescript should be classified he said: "My boy, there are now two of us who know that."

We return to our question: Just how did Shaler learn to see? When Agassiz told him, "That is not right," what did he mean by that? Perhaps if we examine the final paragraph, in which Shaler is describing his "sense of power" *after* he had learned, we can discover something of what his process of learning involved. "I had learned the art of comparing objects," he says. And how does one learn that? There is not much here to go on, but there is at least something in the one example Shaler gives. "I found that one of my species of side-swimmers," he says, "had cycloid scales on one side and ctenoid on the other." Is it possible that one important element in learning to see is the making of distinctions like this one that Shaler "found" between cycloid and ctenoid? Fish scales that were just plain old fish scales before had become differentiated. How? It is a mysterious matter, but this at least we can infer from the evidence Shaler gives us: that whereas at first Shaler was seeing fish scales simply as scales (and "a case for a summary report"), by the end of his learning process he was seeing them as at least two things, cycloid and ctenoid. He had increased his vocabulary. He had gained a "power in dealing with things" which in part at least was a power of language; he had learned to make new distinctions in the classification of fishes by the application of new terms to his experience of seeing.

This process is something like that of reading a difficult passage of literature over and over until you begin to take it in. Shaler learned to "read" his fish—he learned to see words in it, so that what was originally just one more fish in a tray became for him finally a nice intellectual problem suggesting to him the limitations of man-made systems of classifying nature.

This analogy of learning to see with learning to read is made explicit in the next passage you will confront. Here Mark Twain tells how he learned the art of piloting a steamboat on the Mississippi—that is, how he learned to *see* the river. The process of learning to see becomes quite clearly, in Mark Twain's case, a process of "reading" by adding new terms. He looks at the river and he sees a "long slanting line on the face of the water." But this is an inadequate interpretation; it is poor reading. Mr. Bixby, his teacher, translates it for him into pilot-language. "Now, that's a reef. Moreover, it's a bluff reef. There is a solid sand-bar under it that is nearly as straight up and down as the side of a house. . . . If you were to hit it you would knock the boat's brains out." Finally Mark Twain does learn, and the face of the water, he says at the end of our passage, "became a wonderful book—a book that was a dead language to the uneducated passenger, but which told its mind to me without reserve. . . . There never was so wonderful a book written by man. . . ."

That last sentence may be a little ambiguous: Was the book of the river written by man, or not? Evidently not. If it was not

written by man, perhaps you might care to ask who it *was*
written by.

Seeing the Mississippi

MARK TWAIN

At the end of what seemed a tedious while, I had
managed to pack my head full of islands, towns, bars,
"points," and bends; and a curiously inanimate mass of
lumber it was, too. However, inasmuch as I could shut my eyes
and reel off a good long string of these names without leaving
out more than ten miles of river in every fifty, I began to feel
that I could take a boat down to New Orleans if I could make
her skip those little gaps. But of course my complacency could
hardly get started enough to lift my nose a trifle into the air,
before Mr. Bixby would think of something to fetch it down
again. One day he turned on me suddenly with this settler:

"What is the shape of Walnut Bend?"

He might as well have asked me my grandmother's
opinion of protoplasm. I reflected respectfully, and then said I
didn't know it had any particular shape. My gun-powdery
chief went off with a bang, of course, and then went on loading
and firing until he was out of adjectives.

I had learned long ago that he only carried just so many
rounds of ammunition, and was sure to subside into a very
placable and even remorseful old smoothbore as soon as they
were all gone. That word "old" is merely affectionate; he was
not more than thirty-four. I waited. By and by he said:

"My boy, you've got to know the *shape* of the river
perfectly. It is all there is left to steer by on a very dark night.

From *Life on the Mississippi* (1883).

Everything else is blotted out and gone. But mind you, it hasn't the same shape in the night that it has in the day-time."

"How on earth am I ever going to learn it, then?"

"How do you follow a hall at home in the dark? Because you know the shape of it. You can't see it."

"Do you mean to say that I've got to know all the million trifling variations of shape in the banks of this interminable river as well as I know the shape of the front hall at home?"

"On my honor, you've got to know them *better* than any man ever did know the shapes of the halls in his own house."

"I wish I was dead!"

"Now I don't want to discourage you, but—"

"Well, pile it on me; I might as well have it now as another time."

"You see, this has got to be learned; there isn't any getting around it. A clear starlight night throws such heavy shadows that, if you didn't know the shape of a shore perfectly, you would claw away from every bunch of timber, because you would take the black shadow of it for a solid cape; and you see you would be getting scared to death every fifteen minutes by the watch. You would be fifty yards from shore all the time when you ought to be within fifty feet of it. You can't see a snag in one of those shadows, but you know exactly where it is, and the shape of the river tells you when you are coming to it. Then there's your pitch-dark night; the river is a very different shape on a pitch-dark night from what it is on a starlight night. All shores seem to be straight lines then, and mighty dim ones, too; and you'd *run* them for straight lines, only you know better. You boldly drive your boat right into what seems to be a solid, straight wall (you knowing very well that in reality there is a curve there), and that wall falls back and makes way for you. Then there's your gray mist. You take a night when there's one of these grisly, drizzly, gray mists, and then there isn't *any* particular shape to a shore. A gray mist would tangle the head of the oldest man that ever lived. Well, then, different kinds of *moonlight* change the shape of the river in different ways. You see—"

"Oh, don't say any more, please! Have I got to learn the shape of the river according to all these five hundred thousand different ways? If I tried to carry all that cargo in my head it would make me stoop-shouldered."

"*No!* you only learn *the* shape of the river; and you learn it with such absolute certainty that you can always steer by the shape that's *in your head,* and never mind the one that's before your eyes."

"Very well, I'll try it; but, after I have learned it, can I depend on it? Will it keep the same form and not go fooling around?"

Before Mr. Bixby could answer, Mr. W. came in to take the watch, and he said:

"Bixby, you'll have to look out for President's Island, and all that country clear away up above the Old Hen and Chickens. The banks are caving and the shape of the shores changing like everything. Why, you wouldn't know the point above 40. You can go up inside the old sycamore snag, now."

So that question was answered. Here were leagues of shore changing shape. My spirits were down in the mud again. Two things seemed pretty apparent to me. One was, that in order to be a pilot a man had got to learn more than any one man ought to be allowed to know; and the other was, that he must learn it all over again in a different way every twenty-four hours. . . .

It was plain that I had got to learn the shape of the river in all the different ways that could be thought of—upside down, wrong end first, inside out, fore-and-aft, and "thort-ships"—and then know what to do on gray nights when it hadn't any shape at all. So I set about it. In the course of time I began to get the best of this knotty lesson, and my self-complacency moved to the front once more. Mr. Bixby was all fixed, and ready to start it to the rear again. He opened on me after this fashion:

"How much water did we have in the middle crossing at Hole-in-the-Wall, trip before last?"

I considered this an outrage. I said:

"Every trip, down and up, the leadsmen are singing through that tangled place for three-quarters of an hour on a stretch. How do you reckon I can remember such a mess as that?"

"My boy, you've got to remember it. You've got to remember the exact spot and the exact marks the boat lay in when we had the shoalest water, in every one of the five hundred shoal places between St. Louis and New Orleans; and you mustn't get the shoal soundings and marks of one trip mixed up with the shoal soundings and marks of another, either, for they're not often twice alike. You must keep them separate."

When I came to myself again, I said:

"When I get so that I can do that, I'll be able to raise the dead, and then I won't have to pilot a steamboat to make a living. I want to retire from this business. I want a slush-bucket and a brush; I'm only fit for a roustabout. I haven't got brains enough to be a pilot; and if I had I wouldn't have strength enough to carry them around, unless I went on crutches."

"Now drop that! When I say I'll learn* a man the river, I mean it. And you can depend on it, I'll learn him or kill him."

There was no use in arguing with a person like this. I promptly put such a strain on my memory that by and by even the shoal water and the countless crossing-marks began to stay with me. But the result was just the same. I never could more than get one knotty thing learned before another presented itself. Now I had often seen pilots gazing at the water and pretending to read it as if it were a book; but it was

* "Teach" is not in the river vocabulary. [Twain's note.]

a book that told me nothing. A time came at last, however, when Mr. Bixby seemed to think me far enough advanced to bear a lesson on water-reading. So he began:

"Do you see that long, slanting line on the face of the water? Now, that's a reef. Moreover, it's a bluff reef. There is a solid sand-bar under it that is nearly as straight up and down as the side of a house. There is plenty of water close up to it, but mighty little on top of it. If you were to hit it you would knock the boat's brains out. Do you see where the line fringes out at the upper end and begins to fade away?"

"Yes, sir."

"Well, that is a low place; that is the head of the reef. You can climb over there, and not hurt anything. Cross over, now, and follow along close under the reef—easy water there—not much current."

I followed the reef along till I approached the fringed end. Then Mr. Bixby said:

"Now get ready. Wait till I give the word. She won't want to mount the reef; a boat hates shoal water. Stand by—wait—*wait*—keep her well in hand. *Now* cramp her down! Snatch her! snatch her!"

He seized the other side of the wheel and helped to spin it around until it was hard down, and then we held it so. The boat resisted, and refused to answer for a while, and next she came surging to starboard, mounted the reef, and sent a long, angry ridge of water foaming away from her bows.

"Now watch her; watch her like a cat, or she'll get away from you. When she fights strong and the tiller slips a little, in a jerky, greasy sort of way, let up on her a trifle; it is the way she tells you at night that the water is too shoal; but keep edging her up, little by little, toward the point. You are well up on the bar now; there is a bar under every point, because the water that comes down around it forms an eddy and allows the sediment to sink. Do you see those fine lines on the face of the water that branch out like the ribs of a fan? Well, those are little reefs; you want to just miss the ends of them, but run them pretty close. Now look out—look out! Don't you crowd that slick, greasy-looking place; there ain't nine feet there; she won't stand it. She begins to smell it; look sharp, I tell you! Oh, blazes, there you go! Stop the starboard wheel! Quick! Ship up to back! Set her back!"

The engine bells jingled and the engines answered promptly, shooting white columns of steam far aloft out of the 'scape-pipes, but it was too late. The boat had "smelt" the bar in good earnest; the foamy ridges that radiated from her bows suddenly disappeared, a great dead swell came rolling forward, and swept ahead of her, she careened far over to larboard, and went tearing away toward the shore as if she were about scared to death. We were a good mile from where we ought to have been when we finally got the upper hand of her again.

During the afternoon watch the next day, Mr. Bixby asked me if I knew how to run the next few miles. I said:

"Go inside the first snag above the point, outside the next one, start out from the lower end of Higgins's woodyard, make a square crossing, and—"

"That's all right. I'll be back before you close up on the next point."

But he wasn't. He was still below when I rounded it and entered upon a piece of the river which I had some misgivings about. I did not know that he was hiding behind a chimney to see how I would perform. I went gaily along, getting prouder and prouder, for he had never left the boat in my sole charge such a length of time before. I even got to "setting" her and letting the wheel go entirely, while I vaingloriously turned my back and inspected the stern marks and hummed a tune, a sort of easy indifference which I had prodigiously admired in Bixby and other great pilots. Once I inspected rather long, and when I faced to the front again my heart flew into my mouth so suddenly that if I hadn't clapped my teeth together I should have lost it. One of those frightful bluff reefs was stretching its deadly length right across our bows! My head was gone in a moment; I did not know which end I stood on; I gasped and could not get my breath; I spun the wheel down with such rapidity that it wove itself together like a spider's web; the boat answered and turned square away from the reef, but the reef followed her! I fled, but still it followed, still it kept—right across my bows! I never looked to see where I was going, I only fled. The awful crash was imminent. Why didn't that villain come? If I committed the crime of ringing a bell I might get thrown overboard. But better that than kill the boat. So in blind desperation, I started such a rattling "shivaree" down below as never had astounded an engineer in this world before, I fancy. Amidst the frenzy of the bells the engines began to back and fill in a curious way, and my reason forsook its throne—we were about to crash into the woods on the other side of the river. Just then Mr. Bixby stepped calmly into view on the hurricane-deck. My soul went out to him in gratitude. My distress vanished; I would have felt safe on the brink of Niagara with Mr. Bixby on the hurricane-deck. He blandly and sweetly took his toothpick out of his mouth between his fingers, as if it were a cigar—we were just in the act of climbing an overhanging big tree, and the passengers were scudding astern like rats—and lifted up these commands to me ever so gently:

"Stop the starboard! Stop the larboard! Set her back on both!"

The boat hesitated, halted, pressed her nose among the boughs a critical instant, then reluctantly began to back away.

"Stop the larboard! Come ahead on it! Stop the starboard! Come ahead on it! Point her for the bar!"

I sailed away as serenely as a summer's morning. Mr. Bixby came in and said, with mock simplicity:

"When you have a hail, my boy, you ought to tap the big bell three times before you land, so that the engineers can get ready."

I blushed under the sarcasm, and said I hadn't had any hail.

"Ah! Then it was for wood, I suppose. The officer of the watch will tell you when he wants to wood up."

I went on consuming, and said I wasn't after wood.

"Indeed? Why, what could you want over here in the bend, then? Did you ever know of a boat following a bend up-stream at this stage of the river?"

"No, sir—and *I* wasn't trying to follow it. I was getting away from a bluff reef."

"No, it wasn't a bluff reef; there isn't one within three miles of where you were."

"But I saw it. It was as bluff as that one yonder."

"Just about. Run over it!"

"Do you give it as an order?"

"Yes. Run over it!"

"If I don't, I wish I may die."

"All right; I am taking the responsibility."

I was just as anxious to kill the boat, now, as I had been to save it before. I impressed my orders upon my memory, to be used at the inquest, and made a straight break for the reef. As it disappeared under our bows I held my breath; but we slid over it like oil.

"Now, don't you see the difference? It wasn't anything but a *wind* reef. The wind does that."

"So I see. But it is exactly like a bluff reef. How am I ever going to tell them apart?"

"I can't tell you. It is an instinct. By and by you will just naturally *know* one from the other, but you never will be able to explain why or how you know them apart."

It turned out to be true. The face of the water, in time, became a wonderful book—a book that was a dead language to the uneducated passenger, but which told its mind to me without reserve, delivering its most cherished secrets as clearly as if it uttered them with a voice. And it was not a book to be read once and thrown aside, for it had a new story to tell every day. Throughout the long twelve hundred miles there was never a page that was void of interest, never one that you could leave unread without loss, never one that you would want to skip, thinking you could find higher enjoyment in some other thing. There never was so wonderful a book written by man; never one whose interest was so absorbing, so unflagging, so sparklingly renewed with every reperusal. The passenger who could not read it was charmed with a peculiar sort of faint dimple on its surface (on the rare occasions when he did not overlook it altogether); but to the pilot that was an *italicized* passage; indeed, it was more than that, it was a legend of the largest capitals, with a string of shouting exclamation-points at the end of it, for it meant that a wreck or a rock was buried there that could tear the life out of the strongest vessel that ever floated. It is the faintest and simplest expression the water ever makes, and the most hideous to a pilot's eye. In truth, the passenger who could not read this book saw nothing but all manner of pretty pictures in it, painted by the sun and shaded by the clouds, whereas to the trained eye these were not pictures at all, but the grimmest and most deadearnest of reading-matter.

Scholars of American literature have pointed out that the way Mark Twain described himself as a young man in *Life on the Mississippi* and other "autobiographical" works was decidedly fictitious.* The fact is, they say, Mark Twain early in life knew a lot about the river, and he was never the ignorant fool he later made himself out to be. Would you say that therefore Mark Twain was a liar? Maybe so, but a more sensible remark might be that it suited the writer's purpose to recollect himself in this way, perhaps because the experience of learning to "read" the river becomes more dramatic and amusing if the learner is a foolish innocent. The "I" of the passage we have just read is a *character* in the story, and in this case he apparently

* See, for example, Henry Nash Smith, "Mark Twain as an Interpreter of the Far West: The Structure of *Roughing It*," in *The Frontier in Perspective*, ed. Walker D. Wyman and Clifton B. Kroeber (Madison: The Univeristy of Wisconsin Press, 1957).

bore very little relation to the real-life author who created him.

This suggests still another meaning for our complex phrase, point of view. Part of the point from which you view something is the character of the viewer, the "I" of your story. Naturally you want to make this "I" as true to the experience you are describing as you can. Yet, as we have already said, you can hardly do justice in any case to the richness and variety of your real self at any given moment—much less a moment that happened perhaps years ago. Inevitably you must select, ruling out some things and filling in others with whatever your imagination and your sense of your final purpose can provide. Inevitably you become a character in your own story. You have made yourself over, perhaps not as drastically as Mark Twain did, but certainly somewhat.*

Now to our next job of writing. The languages of the biologist or the river pilot may seem remote to you. But you have some languages of your own: you too "read" the world around you all the time, and some of your reading is very skillful. For example, you may have learned enough about baseball to "read" the way a batter holds his feet as an indication that he may be a sucker for an outside curve, or may be ready to bunt, or whatever. Many people have learned enough about hunting to "read" animal tracks in the woods—a language with hundreds of words in it. Perhaps you know something of an auto mechanic's language, and can "read" certain engine noises as symptomatic of this or that impending disaster. Whatever it is that you know (and it is surely something), this exercise asks you to look at it carefully and tell your reader about an example of your learning.

Directions for Essay 4

Choose a particular area of your knowledge, and describe in detail a particular experience in which you learned to

* This notion is more painstakingly set forth in the author's *Persona: A Style Study for Readers and Writers* (New York: Random House, 1969).

"read." Tell the circumstances: where you were, what you were trying to do, who taught you, what it was you learned. At the end of your theme, say just what you mean by "learning" in the context of this experience.

Treacherous though memory is, it seems to me the chief means we have of discovering how a child's mind works. Only by resurrecting our own memories can we realize how incredibly distorted is the child's vision of the world.

GEORGE ORWELL

Chapter
5
Seeing
School Days

The next four chapters in this series are concerned with learning, with yourself as learner, in school and out. The opportunity we hope to provide is to see yourself as a student, from various points of view, in various terms. We will begin simply enough, with a reminiscence of school days.

The reading this time is taken from a book called *A Walker in the City*, in which the author revisits some scenes of his boyhood in that section of Brooklyn known as Brownsville. Here is the way the book begins:

Every time I go back to Brownsville it is as if I had never been away. From the moment I step off the train at Rockaway Avenue and smell the leak out of the men's room, then the pickles from the stand just below the subway steps, an instant rage comes over me, mixed with dread and some unexpected tenderness. It is over ten years since I left to live in "the city"—everything just out of Brownsville was always "the city." Actually I did not go very far; it was enough that I could leave Brownsville. Yet as I walk those familiarly choked streets at dusk and see the old women sitting in front of the tenements, past and present become each other's faces; I am back where I began.

Whenever we read a piece of writing, we have an experience similar to listening to someone speak. In both cases, words are addressed to us, or to someone else, and we infer from the way the words are used the sort of person who is doing the speaking. Of course, when we are in a situation of being talked to by an actual person, we have many things to rely on in addition to words to increase our understanding, such as the way the speaker gestures, the way his voice rises and falls, the way he raises his eyebrows. In written language we have only words. As you examine the words that the "person speaking" is uttering in this paragraph, what can you tell about him—about the kind of person he is, about his attitudes and personality?

Actually you can tell a good deal, just from the way the language is chosen and arranged. For instance, would you say that this speaker talks like a product typical of this immigrant section of Brooklyn? Or is it rather that, in spite of the tawdriness of the scene he describes, he is in fact using a highly educated voice, a voice of the sort which, were we to encounter it in person, we would describe as intelligent and sensitive? Obviously the second is true, and you can find your evidence in the second sentence. Here the voice describes a decidedly unpretty or "tough" spectacle, and he minces no words, but his response is not a simple or crude affair. Immediately after the men's room and the pickles, which he "sees," like one of our blind men from chapter 3, a complex and well-considered statement of feeling follows: not just rage, but rage "mixed with dread" and "unexpected tenderness." That tenderness is unexpected by the reader too. It is as if the vulgarity of the scene were balanced by the sensibility of the speaker's own mind—perhaps as it has developed since leaving Brownsville. We can see another sort of balance between past and present in the way the paragraph begins and ends: ". . . it

is as if I had never been away" and "I am back where I began."
The same balance appears in a single clause "past and present
become each other's faces." We are listening, in short, to a man
who is in control of his voice.

A few pages later, this man, telling us of his return to his
boyhood community after ten years' absence, begins to speak
of his old school, and that is the subject that particularly
concerns us here:

Brownsville School Days

ALFRED KAZIN

All my early life lies open to my eye within five
city blocks. When I passed the school, I went sick with all my
old fear of it. With its standard New York public-school brown
brick courtyard shut in on three sides of the square and the
pretentious battlements overlooking that cockpit in which I
can still smell the fiery sheen of the rubber ball, it looks like a
factory over which has been imposed the façade of a castle. It
gave me the shivers to stand up in that courtyard again; I felt
as if I had been mustered back into the service of those Friday
morning "tests" that were the terror of my childhood.

It was never learning I associated with that school: only
the necessity to succeed, to get ahead of the others in the daily
struggle to "make a good impression" on our teachers, who
grimly, wearily, and often with ill-concealed distaste watched
against our relapsing into the natural savagery they expected
of Brownsville boys. The white, cool, thinly ruled record book
sat over us from their desks all day long, and had remorselessly

entered into it each day—in blue ink if we had passed, in red ink if we had not—our attendance, our conduct, our "effort," our merits and demerits; and to the last possible decimal point in calculation, our standing in an unending series of "tests"— surprise tests, daily tests, weekly tests, formal mid-term tests, final tests. They never stopped trying to dig out of us whatever small morsel of fact we had managed to get down the night before. We had to prove that we were really alert, ready for anything, always in the race. That white thinly ruled record book figured in my mind as the judgment seat; the very thinness and remote blue lightness of its lines instantly showed its cold authority over me; so much space had been left on each page, columns and columns in which to note down everything about us, implacably and forever. As it lay there on a teacher's desk, I stared at it all day long with such fear and anxious propriety that I had no trouble believing that God, too, did nothing but keep such record books, and that on the final day He would face me with an account in Hebrew letters whose phonetic dots and dashes looked strangely like decimal points counting up my every sinful thought on earth.

All teachers were to be respected like gods, and God Himself was the greatest of all school superintendents. Long after I had ceased to believe that our teachers could see with the back of their heads, it was still understood, by me, that they knew everything. They were the delegates of all visible and invisible power on earth—of the mothers who waited on the stoops every day after three for us to bring home tales of our daily triumphs; of the glacially remote Anglo-Saxon principal, whose very name was King; of the incalculably important Superintendent of Schools who would someday rubberstamp his name to the bottom of our diplomas in grim acknowledgment that we had, at last, given satisfaction to him, to the Board of Superintendents, and to our benefactor the City of New York—and so up and up, to the government of the United States and to the great Lord Jehovah Himself. My belief in teachers' unlimited wisdom and power rested not so much on what I saw in them—how impatient most of them looked, how wary—but on our abysmal humility, at least in those of us who were "good" boys, who proved by our ready compliance and "manners" that we wanted to get on. The road to a professional future would be shown us only as we pleased *them. Make a good impression the first day of the term, and they'll help you out. Make a bad impression, and you might as well cut your throat.* This was the first article of school folklore, whispered around the classroom the opening day of each term. You made the "good impression" by sitting firmly at your wooden desk, hands clasped; by silence for the greatest part of the live-long day; by standing up obsequiously when it was so expected of you; by sitting down noiselessly when you had answered a question; by "speaking nicely," which meant reproducing their painfully exact enunciation; by "showing manners," or an ecstatic submissiveness in all things; by outrageous flattery; by bringing little gifts at Christmas, on their birthdays, and at the end of the term—the well-known significance of these gifts being that they came not from us, but from our parents, whose eagerness in this matter showed a high level of social consideration, and thus raised our standing in turn.

It was not just our quickness and memory that were always being tested. Above all, in that word I could never hear without automatically seeing it raised before me in gold-plated letters, it was our *character*. I always felt anxious when I heard the word pronounced. Satisfactory as my "character" was, on the whole, except when I stayed too long in the playground reading; outrageously satisfactory, as I can see now, the very sound of the word as our teachers coldly gave it out from the end of their teeth, with a solemn weight on each dark syllable, immediately struck my heart cold with fear—they could not believe I really had it. Character was never something you had; it had to be trained in you, like a technique. I was never very clear about it. On our side *character* meant demonstrative obedience; but teachers already had it—how else could they have become teachers? They had it; the aloof Anglo-Saxon principal whom we remotely saw only on ceremonial occasions in the assembly was positively encased in it; it glittered off his bald head in spokes of triumphant light; the President of the United States had the greatest conceivable amount of it. Character belonged to great adults. Yet we were constantly being driven onto it; it was the great threshold we had to cross. *Alfred Kazin, having shown proficiency in his course of studies and having displayed satisfactory marks of character* . . . Thus someday the hallowed diploma, passport to my further advancement in high school. But there—I could already feel it in my bones—they would put me through even more doubting tests of character; and after that, if I should be good enough and bright enough, there would be still more. *Character* was a bitter thing, racked with my endless striving to please. The school—from every last stone in the courtyard to the battlements frowning down at me from the walls—was only the stage for a trial. I felt that the very atmosphere of learning that surrounded us was fake—that every lesson, every book, every approving smile was only a pretext for the constant probing and watching of me, that there was not a secret in me that would not be decimally measured into that white record book. All week long I lived for the blessed sound of the dismissal gong at three o'clock on Friday afternoon.

I was awed by this system, I believed in it, I respected its force. The alternative was "going bad." The school was notoriously the toughest in our tough neighborhood, and the dangers of "going bad" were constantly impressed upon me at home and in school in dark whispers of the "reform school" and in examples of boys who had been picked up for petty thievery, rape, or flinging a heavy ink-well straight into a teacher's face. Behind any failure in school yawned the great abyss of a criminal career. Every refractory attitude doomed you with the sound "Sing Sing." Anything less than absolute perfection in school always suggested to my mind that I might fall out of the daily race, be kept back in the working class forever, or—dared I think of it?—fall into the criminal class itself.

I worked on a hairline between triumph and catastrophe. Why the odds should always have felt so narrow I understood only when I realized how little my parents thought of their own lives. It was not for myself alone that I was expected to shine, but for them—to redeem the constant anxiety of their existence. I was the first American child, their offering to the strange new God; I was to be the monument of their liberation from the shame of being—what they were. And that there was shame in this was a fact that everyone seemed to believe as a matter of course. It was in the gleeful discounting of themselves—what do we know?—with which our parents greeted every fresh victory in our savage competition for "high averages," for prizes, for a few condescending words of official praise from the principal at assembly. It was in the sickening invocation of "Americanism"—the word itself accusing us of everything we apparently were not. Our families and teachers seemed tacitly agreed that we were somehow to be a little ashamed of what we were. Yet it was always hard to say why this should be so. It was certainly not—in Brownsville!—because we were Jews, or simply because we spoke another language at home, or were absent on our holy days. It was rather that a "refined," "correct," "nice" English was required of us at school that we did not naturally speak, and that our teachers could never be quite sure we would keep. This English was peculiarly the ladder of advancement. Every future young lawyer was known by it. Even the Communists and Socialists on Pitkin Avenue spoke it. It was bright and clean and polished. We were expected to show it off like a new pair of shoes. When the teacher sharply called a question out, then your name, you were expected to leap up, face the class, and eject those new words fluently off the tongue.

There was my secret ordeal: I could never say anything except in the most roundabout way; I was a stammerer.

Although I knew all those new words from my private reading—I read walking in the street, to and from the Children's Library on Stone Avenue; on the fire escape and the roof; at every meal when they would let me; read even when I dressed in the morning, propping my book up against the drawers of the bureau as I pulled on my long black stockings—I could never seem to get the easiest words out with the right dispatch, and would often miserably signal from my desk that I did not know the answer rather than get up to stumble and fall and crash on every word. If, angry at always being put down as lazy or stupid, I did get up to speak, the black wooden floor would roll away under my feet, the teacher would frown at me in amazement, and in unbearable loneliness I would hear behind me the groans and laughter: *tuh-tuh-tuh-tuh.*

The word was my agony. The word that for others was so effortless and so neutral, so unburdened, so simple, so exact, I had first to meditate in advance, to see if I could make it, like a plumber fitting together odd lengths and shapes of pipe. I was always preparing words I could speak, storing them away, choosing between them. And often, when the word did come from my mouth in its great and terrible birth, quailing and bleeding as if forced through a thornbush, I would not be able to look the others in the face, and would walk out in the silence, the infinitely echoing silence behind my back, to say it all cleanly back to myself as I walked in the streets. Only when I was alone in the open air, pacing the roof with pebbles in my mouth, as I had read Demosthenes had done to cure himself of stammering; or in the street, where all words seemed to flow from the length of my stride and the color of the houses as I remembered the perfect tranquillity of a phrase in Beethoven's *Romance in F* I could sing back to myself as I walked—only then was it possible for me to speak without the infinite premeditations and strangled silences I toiled through whenever I got up at school to respond with the expected, the exact answer.

It troubled me that I could speak in the fullness of my own voice only when I was alone on the streets, walking about. There was something unnatural about it; unbearably isolated. I was not like the others! I was not like the others! At midday, every freshly shocking Monday noon, they sent me away to a speech clinic in a school in East New York, where I sat in a circle of lispers and cleft palates and foreign accents holding a mirror before my lips and rolling difficult sounds over and over. To be sent there in the full light of the opening week, when everyone else was at school or going about his business, made me feel as if I had been expelled from the great normal body of humanity. I would gobble down my lunch on my way to the speech clinic and rush back to the school in time to make up for the classes I had lost. One day, one unforgettable dread day, I stopped to catch my breath on a corner of Sutter Avenue, near the wholesale fruit markets, where an old drugstore rose up over a great flight of steps. In the window were dusty urns of colored water floating off iron chains; cardboard placards advertising hairnets, Ex-Lax; a great illustrated medical chart headed THE HUMAN FACTORY, which showed the exact course a mouthful of food follows as it falls from chamber to chamber of the body. I hadn't meant to stop there at all, only to catch my breath; but I so hated the speech clinic that I thought I would delay my arrival for a few minutes by eating my lunch on the steps. When I took the sandwich out of my bag, two bitterly hard pieces of hard salami slipped out of my hand and fell through a grate onto a hill of dust below the steps. I remember how sickeningly vivid an odd thread of hair looked on the salami, as if my lunch were turning stiff with death. The factory whistles called their short, sharp blasts stark through the middle of noon, beating at me where I sat outside the city's magnetic circle. I had never known, I knew instantly I would never in my heart again submit to, such wild passive despair as I felt at that moment, sitting on the steps before THE HUMAN FACTORY, where little robots gathered and shoveled the food from chamber to chamber of the body. They had put me out into the streets, I thought to myself; with their mirrors and their everlasting pulling at me to imitate their effortless bright speech and their stupefaction that a boy could stammer and stumble on every other English word he carried in his head, they had put me out into the streets, had left me high and dry on the steps of that drugstore staring at the remains of my lunch turning black and grimy in the dust.

Now you are ready to write your own reminiscence of your own school days. Your memories are perhaps not so unhappy as Kazin's, and they are probably different from his in many other ways. But you have two problems, as a writer, that you share with him, and that you must consider carefully as you write.

The first is the matter of your own speaking voice, that person that you become as you address yourself to your reader. This is the same issue we mentioned in relation to Mark Twain's innocent mask in chapter 4, and the general question of how an "I" is to be dramatized. You may not want to adopt the kind of voice that Kazin uses, with that tough-and-tender vocabulary we mentioned in his opening paragraph. But you must more or less consciously choose *some* sort of voice, some speaking personality, to express what you have to say, and you must try to keep that voice consistent from sentence to sentence and paragraph to paragraph. You can write a funny reminiscence if you want, but, if you do, don't try to end with some solemn conclusion that changes your tone. If you decide you're going to speak in an informal, easy sort of way (as in this very sentence, with its contraction and use of the second person), do not abruptly alter your mode of address to a more pontifical guise (as in this part of this sentence). Obviously your teacher will expect from you, whatever your decision, a reasonably mature speaking voice worthy of a student in college.

The second problem you share with Kazin, and a serious one in every theme, is the problem of deciding just how much you can say within your limits of space. You won't be writing anywhere near as long an article as his, and you must certainly restrict the area of experience you choose accordingly. If you try to talk about your school days *in general,* then clearly your writing will be general, and probably dull. The most useful device for overcoming this difficulty is the one Kazin himself employs near the end of his reminiscence: he tells in detail about something that happened to him. Reread the story of the salami and The Human Factory to see how he does it. This is not simply an account of an incidental occurrence, of course. It has a meaning for him; he has made it stand for or signify a whole attitude toward his school days, his teachers, his loneliness. In some similar way, you would be wise to select a *particular incident* that once happened to you, and that you can use to stand for *your* remembrance of a certain time of your life. You will be *seeing* this incident, then, as meaningful for you.

Directions for Essay 5

Write a description of your own school days in which you focus on a particular incident, in class or elsewhere, that seems to you to dramatize your attitude toward your school and your teachers at a particular period of your life.

We wish to make the ego the object of our study, our own ego. But how can we do that? The ego is the subject par excellence, how can it become the object? There is no doubt, however, that it can. The ego can take itself as object, it can treat itself like any other object, observe itself, criticize itself, and do Heaven knows what besides with itself.

FREUD

Chapter
6

Seeing School as They-and-Me

The next passage for reading is taken from a talk delivered to a group of prospective teachers by a psychologist and counselor of college students. This talk, though composed almost a quarter century ago, anticipates a problem that has become acute in very recent years—the feeling among so many young people of being victims in a vast educational machine that cares little about them as people. But the voice you will be hearing is a far different voice from the serious, sensitive one you heard in Kazin. This voice is easy, informal, colloquial—the voice of a *talker* speaking to a group of interested intelligent people on a difficult subject, but determined not to be too solemn about it. Most of his language accordingly is simple, as in conversation. "I am going to draw a kind of chart," he announces at the end of the first paragraph, and notice that it's not just a chart alone that he's going to draw, but "a kind of chart," reminding us of the modesty of his ambitions. He goes on: ". . . in the hope that it may keep us from becoming utterly lost." This suggests that we will become *somewhat* lost anyway, chart or no chart. It's very relaxing to know that not too much is expected of us.

Conflicts in the Learning Process

WILLIAM G. PERRY, Jr.

What I am going to do is to try to explore how the educational world looks to the student—perhaps, indeed, how the world itself looks. By this I don't mean what he will or can tell you about it; I mean, rather, what his assumptions are and what his frame of reference is, the more or less unconscious basis of his behavior. Here I am launching those tentative suppositions in which one must explore the sea of one's ignorance. I am going to draw a kind of chart in the hope that it may keep us from becoming utterly lost.

When we as children first come into the world and look around to see what the world is made of, we see soon enough that the world is made of They. And what are They like? They tell us, do they not, what we *ought to* do? They tell us our *duty*. They tell us what is *necessary*. And it is necessary to do a lot of things that we don't like in the world, so They say. It is necessary to do a lot of things that are unpleasant. So that this business that They tell us about is by their own account *unpleasant*. So this is the world and its demands.

But now, as I look at this world, I begin to think of my own individuality and separateness, and I say to myself, "Who's Me?" Well, I am little and I am helpless, but I obviously have to be something quite different from all this if I

Reprinted by permission of the publishers from Bernice Brown Cronkhite, editor, *A Handbook for College Teachers: An Informal Guide*. Cambridge, Mass.: Harvard University Press, Copyright, 1950, by The President and Fellows of Harvard College.

am going to have any differentness, any individuality, which seems so precious to me. And what is the opposite to all that They stand for? Why, it is obviously what I *want*. So it follows that my individuality and my integrity, for which I will fight to the death, consists of what I want—that is, of my *wishes*—all of which I associate with the *pleasant:*

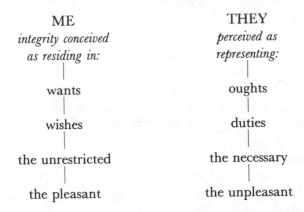

ME *integrity conceived as residing in:*	THEY *perceived as representing:*
wants	oughts
wishes	duties
the unrestricted	the necessary
the pleasant	the unpleasant

Clearly, now, I am faced at once with a number of serious difficulties. In the first place my integrity demands that I get what I want. If I do not, I am not only frustrated, I am much worse than that: I am somehow less Me. On the other hand, a lot of things that I want can be attained only through They, and They disapprove of other things that I want. If I do not give up these tabooed wants and do a certain amount of the unpleasant, then They will not love me any more, and that would be fatal to all my wishes. Furthermore, I may feel in part genuinely fond of They in that They do give me some things I want. Another difficulty is still more confusing. I soon discover, let us say at the age of three or four, or five, that They got me so young, when I was unable to defend myself, that They went and put a little bit of They in Me and I can't get away from it; it keeps nagging me all the time.

The dilemma is very serious indeed, and is made worse by the conflicting nature of my wishes. I wish to be dominant and independent; I wish also to be dependent and loved. However, I blind myself to this internal source of difficulty and concentrate on what seems the external problem of getting what I want and placating They. There are all sorts of attempted solutions to this almost insoluble problem. The most obvious one is the Social Contract of Rousseau—that is, the compromise. In this solution I simply do a number of the things that They say I ought to do, and then I hope that They will leave me alone to go forth and do some of the things that I want. The trouble with this solution is that the compromise never really seems to be accepted by either side; both sides seem to be trying to beat the game and to ask for more. It is a very uneasy situation. I do some of the things that I want to do for a while; then I get a guilty conscience and do some of the things that I ought to do for a while; then I feel frustrated and so I go and do what I want to do, and then I get conscience-stricken again, and back and forth, back and forth, I go. And all this time the sensation keeps piling up that somebody is wasting time.

We might digress for a moment here and look at a curious application of this Social Contract in the educational world. It is perfectly clear to Me, in the educational world, that what They want is for me to be good; what They want is for me to do my duty, which is to sit down and do this studying that I have been given to do. If I do that, their part of the bargain is that They will give me the good grade that I want, so we get the curious formula which you find running throughout education, namely: work through time equals grades. This is a kind of basic moral law. It does not matter what I say on an examination; if I have done the work I should get the grade, and if my roommate, who has done none of the work, reads my notes before the examination and goes in and gets a higher grade than I do, that shows that They are unfair.

We might digress a little further. My integrity, my sense of Meness is bound up with my wishes, and since They invade my integrity with all these "don'ts" and "ought's," and since the Social Contract is not working very well and I am getting a little resentful, it is very natural for me to decide that I really could have everything that I wanted if it were not for They; given half a chance I would prove as omnipotent as I secretly believe myself to be. This feeling, which we have all shared, is exemplified by a student who once said: "I really could cut loose from everything; I could cut loose from my parents and my wife and from everything, just as a friend of mine has done who is now down in Ceylon. I could do that, only I don't think I ought to. I could be really perfectly independent and get· everything that I wanted. I just don't do it because I don't think I *should*. Besides that, of course, I gain such satisfactions from my family." I said, "You mean that if you went to Ceylon you wouldn't have those satisfactions that you want?" He replied, "No." He was still blind to his contradiction. Then suddenly it struck him, and he said, "This is the first time I've ever realized that I couldn't really have everything I wanted if it wasn't for them."

If it is natural and easy for us to engage in this kind of thinking about our omnipotence, we can carry it one step further. I shall bethink me of the future; I shall conjure up an ideal picture of what I shall become. I shall be a doctor, a really great doctor; I shall be so clever that everyone will admire me, and I shall know so much that I can do anything I want. Now it is a highly commendable thing to be a good doctor and to make discoveries that will ease the lot of the human race, and here, you see, is where I satisfy They, especially the They of my own conscience. So here I have an ideal which seems to satisfy both my need for independence or power and my conscience. There is only one trouble with it—the minute that I try to put it into action, They get in my way again; They require that I study German and various aspects of physics and literature which will be really of no use to me. Naturally, it is an invasion of my integrity to study these requirements and somehow I have a terrible time with them. "I won't eat those beans if They tell me to; no matter how good they may be, no matter how fine the dessert, it is not worth the price of my integrity, and I won't do it." Or if my revolt is not as conscious as this, I will simply relegate doing them until "tomorrow."

We had better not digress any more, for we could probably digress forever and still have an over-simple picture of the matter. It is my opinion, anyway, that from the particular point of view of which we have been speaking—that is, the child's point of view—the problems of life are actually insoluble. It has always been my suspicion that Rousseau never quite grew up. Let us go back to the point where we felt that in the midst of all these attempted solutions somebody was wasting time.

It is this very notion of time that is crucial. Until now we have made no mention of time. Time is an aspect of reality, and we have made no mention whatever of reality. To the child there is no such thing as reality directly; there is only what They say is necessary, and even when what They say is necessary or real actually happens, even that appears to be just an "I-told-you-so" of grown-ups. Time, as one aspect of reality, does not apply to Me. In fact Me is at its most omnipotent in the timelessness of tomorrow. One of the most obvious solutions to the dilemma of the Me is to do what I want to do today and do what I ought to do tomorrow. Perhaps it is in large part through this sensation of wasting time that reality first comes into awareness—that I get my first glimpse of just plain fact. It is this stunning revelation of the factual, the notion that I cannot go to Ceylon and have everything that I want, that breaks down utterly the dichotomy of the They and the Me. And here we are on the brink of maturity. For now that this dichotomy is broken down, we can have a look at the frame of reference from which the sensation that I have been wasting time arises. The whole sensation implies a new value system, some wholly different frame of reference in which defending the integrity of my wishes is not what I really want to be doing. Here it is that I discover that the person who has been wasting time is my Self.

It is upon the difference between the Me and the Self that everything that I have to say hinges. The difference is one of essential personal identity; it is a felt difference that concerns who I am—that concerns what makes up, for me, my personal individuality. We have already seen that for the child identity is conceived as consisting of wishes, especially those wishes which the child holds in contradistinction of They. No internal conflict or contradiction is accepted among these wishes; all conflict is projected and seems to be externally imposed. But for the Self wishes suddenly lose their distinctive and individual character. I suddenly perceive that everyone has much the same wishes, and furthermore I see these wishes as an aspect of fact and reality. They then lose their glorious simplicity and can be seen in all the conflict and complexity which is really theirs. For the first time, therefore, I am confronted with the real issue of *choice*. The individuality and integrity of the Self is therefore conceived to reside not in my wishes, but in the act of choosing in the midst of the complexity of reality. This reality consists not only of my wishes, but also of society and of physical limitations, including that of time. Up until now I had confused freedom with independence; now I realize that freedom is not the independence to follow one's wishes, but the act of choice among personal values. And personal values for my Self include not only wishes in the narrow sense of impulses, but also objective purposes in a real world *and* many of those responsibilities and obligations and duties which I have previously seen only as the demands of They. In this new frame of reference it is no longer either a loss of integrity, or an act of masochism, to do something unpleasant; it may be simply useful or productive. And though I still have both my wishes and my "ought's," my integrity is not at issue between them; it is, in fact, expressed in my act of choice whichever way I choose in relation to a particular set of circumstances in reality.

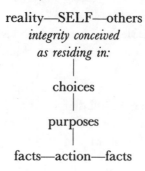

As an illustration we might consider the matter of the language requirement. Almost all colleges and graduate schools have a language requirement, and as students we buck it. It is a great symbol, the language requirement; it is the last great apotheosis of Their incredible and unreasonable demands. When it comes time to sit down and do that German, we read the newspaper, we read *Life,* we sharpen our pencils, we do anything to delay the awful moment. When finally we do get to work, we do just what we feel we are "required" to do: we turn the word-cards over, we translate word by word from this or that, and if nothing comes from all our labors, it is not our fault, it is Theirs; and the fact that nothing ever seems to come out of it just goes to show how right we are. The language requirement appears as a price we are forced to pay for a degree which They withhold. It obviously is not the business of a Me, it is just a requirement of They, and I spend a great deal of time expanding upon its archaism and injustice. From the point of view of the Self, however, the matter looks very different indeed. You have come to this store of your own choice, to buy a certain article, an A.B. or a Ph.D. And how in this store does this article come packaged; in what form does it appear on the counter? It always includes the language requirement. It is not, if you please, a price that you pay, but rather part of the product that you buy. You may not want this accessory, you understand, you may not consider it reasonable, and you may wish that the product came packaged without it; but if the management is not disposed to change the package, you have, in fact, a choice of taking the article or leaving it. If you choose to take it, it is not an invasion of your integrity to fulfill the language requirement; it is, in fact, an expression of your own choice in regard to reality; and because the Self is primarily the chooser, it is an act of Self-expression. Certainly it may be unpleasant or dull, and even frustrating of other purposes that you would like to substitute for it; but for the Self, frustration is not purely an imposition from the outside and a threat to integrity; rather it is one of the conditions of life, because even my own wishes are often incompatible. Hence, dull or not, it can be done with a will.

In the event that you have been subscribing at all to this, you have probably been looking at yourself, if not with alarm, at least with some concern, with the question, "Am I a Me or am I a Self? Am I a child or am I an adult?" I doubt that you will find a ready answer. The question would have been prompted by the way I have been presenting this. I have seemed to imply that a person is either a child or an adult, but this is because such things as authority, necessity, and the unpleasant are so sharply different in quality when looked at from the two points of view that there are really no in-betweens; it is an all-or-none proposition. The two frames of reference are separate, distinct, and self-contained, but what makes growth into maturity look like a gradual thing is, I think, first that we take the point of view of Self in one area of life at a time and, second, that even in those areas in which we have attained it, it is notoriously unstable. A student, for instance, may attain a mature frame of reference in his social relationships and remain a child in his school work. He may feel and act as an adult in his summer job and in the fall drag his feet, as a pupil, reluctantly to school. He may feel and act as an adult away from home, but when he returns to the family that treats him as a child, he will feel like one. It is this jumping back and forth from one frame of reference to an-

other that is the basis, I believe, of the instability of ado-
lescence. Of course it stays with us, to a degree, all our lives.

So far I have painted the frame of reference of the Self as
so much more comfortable and desirable that this critical
instability may seem strange. Let us have a look at a few of its
discomforts. Being a Self is a very risky and frightening
business. As a Me I still have claims on that day when things
go wrong in life. When I fail, when I am disappointed, when I
am hurt, I can call on Them for comfort, for love, for
reassurance, for protection. If I am a Self, I no longer have
these claims in anything like the same degree. In fact I am
alone, and I have not yet learned that to be alone, as all
human beings are, is not necessarily to be lonely. Hardest of
all, I must, to be a Self, allow my wishes, my omnipotence, and
my fantasies to suffer real defeats in the face of reality. I may
never be a really great doctor, and to be even a mediocre one,
or even a failure, I must sweat. Even if I turn out to have
ability and have worked hard, just plain circumstances may
defeat me. Can I stand this without the compensation of Their
sympathy and support, without being able to demand that
They play fair? And deeper down than any of this, can I really
trust my Self? If I try to rely on choice instead of upon the
compulsions of "ought's" and "must's," will I ever get
anything done?

We might take this last question and see how the fear
operates to tip us out of the mature frame of reference.
Suppose that I am approaching my academic work, and the
language requirement too, with all kinds of maturity. I have
kept in mind my own choice; I have come to this institution
because I chose to; I accept the language requirement as an
aspect of reality; I accept the notion that time applies to me;
and I choose, therefore, to do the language requirement now
rather than tomorrow. I am doing my German, and my
roommate comes in and asks me to make a fourth at bridge.
Now I enjoy bridge; furthermore I haven't played for quite
some time; furthermore I have been working very hard. I

deserve (what frame of reference does that word come from?) a bit of change, a little relaxation. I am sorely tempted. Suddenly I am afraid. I am afraid that I will go and play bridge and not get that language requirement done. I suddenly lose confidence in the Self to choose wisely. I cannot say to my roommate or to myself, "That sounds nice, but I want to get this German done." I cannot voice a simple preference. Instead, I say, "No, I really *ought* to do my German, I really *must* get it done." Now understand me, it looks as if I have not capitulated. I have not said to myself that I can do the German "tomorrow" and I have not gone off to play bridge. But I have capitulated. I have lost confidence in my own capacity to choose, and I have called upon the "ought's" and the "should's" and the "must's" to compel me, to do the deciding for me; and in the next hour, how I will resent it! I have set They up again as my masters, and how I will buck them! I will feel frustrated, I will think about the bridge, and somehow I will defeat my efforts to learn anything. Of course I may be able to get something done for a while by glorying in a kind of masochistic righteousness, but I won't keep it up for long. My spell of self-righteousness will only give me the excuse for taking the whole week end off. From the mature point of view it would have been better had my Self actually chosen to play bridge and to deal with the consequences. I am not arguing against the value of a conscience; I am saying that if we set up the conscience as our compulsive authority instead of as our guide, then we may react as children toward it. To rely entirely upon its compulsion is to surrender the integrity of the Self, to abnegate the function of choice. Until one has had a little experience with the Self, it is hard to believe that we, as people, could really *prefer* to do our work. We say, "I have to drive myself to work." Who is driving whom here? Self-expression is the act of doing what we as *whole* people prefer.

Perhaps we can turn now to the subject of education. I was talking with a student the other day who relied so heavily upon his conscience and upon his parents that though he had the intentions of doing college work, he could not see them as his own. Whenever he told himself that he ought to get to work, he sounded to himself so much like his parents that he resisted his own statements. There was a constant strife between the parent in him, who was trying to make him do things, and the child in him, who was in revolt. Things had gotten a little pressing just before examinations, and he had begun to do a little work. He had decided, he said, that the only trouble with him was that he had no incentive. "But recently," he said, "I've had a lot of incentive; in fact I can't remember being so incensed in all my life."

What I am trying to say is that being incensed may be the normal and appropriate state of mind of the young while being educated. Education is the way that we get at them. We force the culture upon them, the "do's" and the "don'ts" and the "ought's" and the "must's," and when they start doing these, can they eagerly espouse them and keep their integrity, or must they resist to live? Watch them. They go on slow-down strikes and become slow readers. They bewilder themselves by their "laziness." They appeal to you, in conscience-stricken despair. And when they do their work, is their main purpose to learn something or to placate you? It is very profitable and enlightening to look at the act of studying as the process of placating authority in the educational world.

Does this sound extreme? I remember when I first went into the business of helping students to study better, more efficiently and all that. I assumed, of course, that everybody wants to be efficient—that is, to get the same results with the least effort—and for all I know this still may be a perfectly reasonable assumption. When a student came to me, I would try to show him how to be efficient. He would say, "Here are my notes. I take lots of notes. I don't really know what is the matter, I'm not getting anywhere, that's all. I've been working and working and working, but I don't get the grades." Well, he would have plenty of notes, all right, stacks of them, all very neatly arranged, and most of them copied right out of the book; so I would show him, as kindly as possible, how inefficient all this was, how he had written and written but hadn't learned a thing. And I would show him how to learn much more and to do about one-fourth of all that copy work, and then he would say, "I don't know why I didn't think of that before; why that's marvelous! Thank you so much, sir." And he would run off. In a few weeks I'd see him again and say, "How are you getting on these days?" And there would be that same mass of verbatim notes. And while I sat there, feeling that wave of the teacher's despair, the student would say, "I tried your method, sir, really I did [whose method?], but I don't know, really, sir, it just seems *better* this way."

Now the student was right. I had been trying to give him an efficient way of learning something, whereas he already had a very efficient way of satisfying his conscience, which was what he was mainly trying to do. You cannot imagine a more efficient way to satisfy your conscience than sitting for hours and writing out those notes. The note goes from the book up one finger and one arm, and across the shoulders, and down the other arm onto the paper, and your mind and heart and soul can be off on something else more pleasant. No extra effort at all. Such a method for such a student is admirably designed to fit his purposes. Do you suppose, as a teacher, that your main problem will be your students' stupidity? Or does it begin to seem as if your main problem might be the extraordinary wisdom of their resistance? . . .

We have pointed out that the tone of voice in this article is easy, informal, conversational. We could examine the second paragraph as an example, and conclude that here the vocabulary and sentence structure are even childlike. Short words, little questions with little answers. But already, in that second paragraph, disguised behind the childish repetitions, a sort of "key term" appears, a piece of vocabulary that looks childish and vague but is in fact used in an almost technical sense. This is, of course, the term "They," carefully capitalized, to point as a child might point to parents, teachers, and adults generally in all their awful authority.

In the next paragraph comes a corollary key term: Me. These two words, together with "integrity" and a good many others that follow, make up a vocabulary about teaching and learning. Here is a writer (or talker) who is describing the relation of the young to their elders, particularly to their schoolteachers, and he is using a particular set of terms to do it. Does any of what he is saying offer a fresh way of seeing yourself as a schoolboy or girl? Can you find, in the language of this easy-talking psychologist, some terms that could be applied to your situation as you described it in essay 5?

As you reread this speech, then, make a list of some of these key terms that Perry uses in his own special sense, like Me-They and "integrity." When you have finished, you should be in a position to resee your school days.

Directions for Essay 6

Rewrite your school days by reseeing your incident of essay 5, using some of Perry's key terms. What happens to your school days when you change your terms in this way? Do your school days change too?

It is not possible to spend any prolonged period visiting public school classrooms without being appalled by the mutilation visible everywhere—mutilation of spontaneity, of joy in learning, of pleasure in creating, of sense of self.

CHARLES E. SILBERMAN

Chapter
7

Seeing School as Nightmare

A great many experts have held forth on the subject of education in the past decade or so, and most of them have been gloomy. High schools have been particularly under attack, and the growth of "student-centered" theories of teaching suggests our dissatisfaction with traditional classroom behavior. You, the student everybody is talking for, might pause to consider what has been happening to you and how you feel about it. The article that follows offers some terms for one kind of answer.

As you read this article by an anthropologist, keep in mind two tasks. One is simply to identify the "nightmare" he claims students learn in school. The other is to ask yourself whether this nightmare relates to you and your experience as a student, either specifically in the incident you related for essay 5, or generally in other incidents you might now care to recollect.

American Schoolrooms: Learning the Nightmare

JULES HENRY

School is an institution for drilling children in cultural orientations. Educators have attempted to free the school from drill, but have failed because they have always chosen the most obvious "enemy" to attack. Furthermore, with every enemy destroyed, new ones are installed among the old fortifications that are the enduring contradictory maze of the culture. Educators think that when they have made arithmetic or spelling into a game; made it unnecessary for children to "sit up straight"; defined the relation between teacher and children as democratic; and introduced plants, fish, and hamsters into schoolrooms, they have settled the problem of drill. They are mistaken.

The paradox of the human condition is expressed more in education than elsewhere in human culture, because learning to learn has been and continues to be *Homo sapiens'* most formidable evolutionary task. Although it is true that mammals, as compared to birds and fishes, have to learn so much that it is difficult to say by the time we get to chimpanzees which behavior is inborn and which is learned, the learning task has become so enormous for man that today, education, along with survival, constitutes a major preoccupation. In all the fighting over education we are simply saying that after a million years of struggling to become human, we are not yet satisfied that we have mastered the fundamental human task, learning.

Another learning problem inherent in the human condition is this: We must conserve culture while changing it, we must always be *more* sure of surviving than of adapting. Whenever a new idea appears, our first concern as *animals* must be that it does not kill us; then, and only then, can we look at it from other points of view. In general, primitive people solved this problem simply by walling their children off from new possibilities by educational methods that, largely through fear, so narrowed the perceptual sphere that nontraditional ways of viewing the world became unthinkable.

The function of education has never been to free the mind and the spirit of man, but to bind them. To the end that the mind and spirit of his children should never escape, *Homo sapiens* has wanted acquiescence, not originality, from his offspring. It is natural that this should be so, for where every man is unique there is no society, and where there is no society there can be no man. Contemporary American educators think they want creative children, yet it is an open question as to what they expect these children to create. If all through school the young were provoked to question the Ten Commandments, the sanctity of revealed religion, the foundations of patriotism, the profit motive, the two-party system, monogamy, the laws of incest, and so on, we would have more creativity than we could handle. In teaching our children to accept fundamentals of social relationships and religious beliefs without question we follow the ancient highways of the human race.

American classrooms, like educational institutions anywhere, express the values, preoccupations, and fears found in the culture as a whole. School has no choice; it must train the children to fit the culture as it is. School can give training in skills; it cannot teach creativity. Since the creativity that *is* encouraged—as in science and mathematics, for example—will always be that which satisfies the cultural drives at the time, all the American school can do is nurture that creativity when it appears.

Creative intellect is mysterious, devious, and irritating.

An intellectually creative child may fail in social studies, for example, simply because he cannot understand the stupidities he is taught to believe as "fact." He may even end up agreeing with his teachers that he is "stupid" in social studies. He will not be encouraged to play among new social systems, values, and relationships, if for no other reason than that the social studies teachers will perceive such a child as a poor student. Furthermore, such a child will simply be unable to fathom the absurdities that seem transparent *truth* to the teacher. What idiot believes in the "law of supply and demand," for example? But the children who do, tend to *become* idiots; and learning to be an idiot is part of growing up! Or, as Camus put it, learning to be *absurd*. Thus the intellectually creative child who finds it impossible to learn to think the absurd the truth, who finds it difficult to accept absurdity as a way of life, usually comes to think himself stupid.

Schools have therefore never been places for the stimulation of young minds; they are the central conserving force of the culture, and if we observe them closely they will tell us much about the cultural pattern that binds us.

Much of what I am now going to say pivots on the inordinate capacity of a human being to learn more than one thing at a time. A child writing the word "August" on the board, for example, is not only learning the word "August," but also how to hold the chalk without making it squeak, how to write clearly, how to keep going even though the class is tittering at his slowness, how to appraise the glances of the children in order to know whether he is doing it right or wrong. If a classroom can be compared to a communications system—a flow of messages between teacher (transmitter) and pupils (receivers)—it is instructive to recall another characteristic of communications systems applicable to classrooms: their inherent tendency to generate *noise*. *Noise*, in communications theory, applies to all those random fluctuations of the system that cannot be controlled, the sounds that are not part of the message. The striking thing about the child is that along with his "messages about spelling" he learns all the noise in the system also. But—and mark this well—it is *not* primarily the message (the spelling) that constitutes the most important subject matter to be learned, but the noise! The most significant cultural learnings—primarily the cultural drives—are communicated as *noise.* Let us see the system operate in some of the contemporary suburban classrooms my students and I studied over a period of six years.

It is March 17 and the children are singing songs from Ireland and her neighbors. The teacher plays on the piano, while the children sing. While some children sing, a number of them hunt in the index, find a song belonging to one of Ireland's neighbors, and raise their hands in order that they may be called on to name the next song. The singing is of that pitchless quality always heard in elementary school classrooms. The teacher sometimes sings through a song first, in her off-key, weakishly husky voice.

The usual reason for this kind of song period is that the children are "broadened" while they learn something about music and singing. But what the children in fact learn about singing is to sing like everybody else. (This phenomenon—the standard, elementary school pitchlessness of the English-speaking world—was impressive enough for D. H. Lawrence to mention it in *Lady Chatterley's Lover.* The difficulty in achieving true pitch is so pervasive among us that missionaries carry it with them to distant jungles, teaching the natives to sing hymns off key. Hence on Sundays we would hear our Pilagá Indian friends, all of them excellent musicians in the Pilagá scale, carefully copy the missionaries by singing Anglican hymns, translated into Pilagá, off key exactly as sharp or as flat as the missionaries sang.) Thus one of the first things a child with a good ear learns in elementary school is to be musically stupid; he learns to doubt or to scorn his innate musical capacities.

But possibly more important than this is the use to which teacher and pupils put the lesson in ways not related at all to singing or to Ireland and her neighbors. To the teacher this was an opportunity to let the children somehow share the social aspects of the lesson with her. The consequence was distraction from singing as the children hunted in the index, and the net result was to activate the children's drives toward competition, achievement, and dominance. In this way the song period was scarcely a lesson in singing, but rather one in extorting the maximal benefit for the Self from *any* situation.

The first lesson a child has to learn when he comes to school is that lessons are not what they seem. He must then forget this and act as if they were. This is the first step toward "school mental health"; it is also the first step in becoming absurd. The second lesson is to put the teachers' and students' criteria in place of his own. The child must learn that the proper way to sing is tunelessly and not the way he hears the music; that the proper way to paint is the way the teacher says, not the way he sees it; that the proper attitude is not pleasure, but competitive horror at the success of his classmates, and so on. And these lessons must be so internalized that he will fight his parents if they object. The early schooling process is not successful unless it has produced in the child an acquiescence in its criteria, unless the child *wants* to think the way school has taught him to think. What we see in kindergarten and the early years of school is the pathetic surrender of babies. How could it be otherwise?

Now nothing so saps self-confidence as alienation from the Self. It would follow that school, the chief agent in the process, must try to provide the children with "ego support," for culture tries to remedy the ills it creates. Hence the effort to give children recognition in our schools. Hence the conversion of the songfest into an exercise in Self-realization. That anything essential was nurtured in this way is an open question, for the kind of individuality that was recognized as the children picked titles out of the index was mechanical, without a creative dimension, and under the strict control of the teacher. In short, the school metamorphoses the child, giving it the kind of Self the school can manage, and then proceeds to minister to the Self it has made.

We can see this at work in another example:

> The observer is just entering her fifth-grade classroom for the observation period. The teacher says, "Which one of you nice, polite boys would like to take [the observer's] coat and hang it up?" From the waving hands, it would seem that all would like to claim the honor. The teacher chooses one child, who takes the observer's coat. . . . The teacher conducted the arithmetic lessons mostly by asking, "Who would like to tell the answer to the next problem?" This question was followed by the usual large and agitated forest of hands, with apparently much competition to answer.

What strike us here are the precision with which the teacher was able to mobilize the potentialities in the boys for the proper social behavior, and the speed with which they responded. The large number of waving hands proves that most of the boys have already become absurd; but they have no choice. Suppose they sat there frozen?

A skilled teacher sets up many situations in such a way that *a negative attitude can be construed only as treason.* The function of questions like, "Which one of you nice, polite boys would like to take [the observer's] coat and hang it up?" is to bind the children into absurdity—to compel them to acknowledge that absurdity is existence, to acknowledge that it is better to exist absurd than not to exist at all. The reader will have observed that the question is not put, "Who *has* the answer to the next problem?" but, "Who *would like to tell*" it. What at one time in our culture was phrased as a challenge to skill in arithmetic, becomes here an invitation to group participation. The essential issue is that *nothing is but what it is made to be by the alchemy of the system.*

In a society where competition for the basic cultural goods is a pivot of action, people cannot be taught to love one another. It thus becomes necessary for the school to teach children how to hate, and without appearing to do so, for our culture cannot tolerate the idea that babes should hate each other. How does the school accomplish this ambiguity? Obviously through fostering competition itself, as we can see in an incident from a fifth-grade arithmetic lesson.

Boris had trouble reducing 12/16 to the lowest terms, and could only get as far as 6/8. The teacher asked him quietly if that was as far as he could reduce it. She suggested he "think." Much heaving up and down and waving of hands by the other children, all frantic to correct him. Boris pretty unhappy, probably mentally paralyzed. The teacher, quiet, patient, ignores the others and concentrates with look and voice on Boris. After a minute or two, she turns to the class and says, "Well, who can tell Boris what the number is?" A forest of hands appears, and the teacher calls Peggy. Peggy says that four may be divided into the numerator and the denominator.

Boris's failure has made it possible for Peggy to succeed; his misery is the occasion for her rejoicing. This is the standard condition of the contemporary American elementary school. To a Zuñi, Hopi, or Dakota Indian, Peggy's performance would seem cruel beyond belief, for competition, the wringing of success from somebody's failure, is a form of torture foreign to those noncompetitive cultures. Yet Peggy's action seems natural to us; and so it is. How else would you run our world?

Looked at from Boris's point of view, the nightmare at the blackboard was, perhaps, a lesson in controlling himself so that he would not fly shrieking from the room under enormous public pressure. Such experiences force every man reared in our culture, over and over again, night in, night out, even at the pinnacle of success, to dream not of success, but of failure. In school the external nightmare is internalized for life. Boris was not learning arithmetic only; he was learning the *essential nightmare also. To be successful in our culture one must learn to dream of failure.*

When we say that "culture teaches drives and values" we do not state the case quite precisely. We should say, rather, that culture (and especially the school) provides the occasions in which drives and values are *experienced in events* that strike us with *overwhelming and constant force.* To say that culture "teaches" puts the matter too mildly. Actually culture invades and infests the mind as an obsession. If it does not, it will be powerless to withstand the impact of critical differences, to fly in the face of contradiction, to so engulf the mind that the world is seen only as the culture decrees it shall be seen, to compel a person to be absurd. The central emotion in obsession is fear, and the central obsession in education is fear of failure. In school, one becomes absurd through being afraid; but paradoxically, *only by remaining absurd can one feel free from fear.*

Let us see how absurdity is reinforced: consider this spelling lesson in a fourth-grade class.

The children are to play "spelling baseball," and they have lined up to be chosen for the two teams. There is much noise, but the teacher quiets it. She has selected a boy and a girl and sent them to the front of the room as team captains to choose their teams. As the boy and girl pick the children to form their teams, each child takes a seat in orderly succession around the room. Apparently they know the game well. Now Tom, who has not yet been chosen, tries to call attention to himself in order to be chosen. Dick shifts his position to be more in the direct line of vision of the choosers, so that he may not be overlooked. He seems quite anxious. Jane, Tom, Dick, and one girl whose name the observer does not know are the last to be chosen. The teacher even has to remind the choosers that Dick and Jane have not been chosen. . . .

The teacher now gives out words for the children to spell, and they write them on the board. [Each word is a pitched ball, and each correctly spelled word is a base hit. The children move around the room from base to base as their teammates spell the words correctly.] The outs seem to increase in frequency as each side gets near the children chosen last. The children have great difficulty spelling "August." As they make mistakes, those in the seats say, "No!" The teachers says, "Man on third." As a child at the board stops and thinks, the teacher says, "There's a time limit; you can't take too long, honey." At last, after many children fail on "August" one child gets it right and returns, grinning with pleasure, to her seat. . . . The motivation level in this game seems terrific. All the children seem to watch the board, to know what's right and wrong, and seem quite keyed up. There is no lagging in moving from base to base. The child who is now writing "Thursday" stops to think after the first letter, and the children snicker. He stops after another letter. More snickers. He gets the word wrong. There are frequent signs of joy from the children when their side is right.

"Spelling baseball" is an effort to take the "weariness, the fever, and the fret" out of spelling by absurdly transforming it into a competitive game. Children are usually good competitors, though they may never become good spellers; and although they may never learn to *spell* success, they know what it *is*, how to go after it, and how it feels not to have it. A competitive game is indicated when children are failing, because the drive to succeed in the *game* may carry them to victory over the subject matter. But once a spelling lesson is cast in the form of a game of baseball a great variety of *noise* enters the system; because the sounds of *baseball* (the baseball "messages") cannot but be *noise* in a system intended to communicate *spelling*. If we reflect that one could not settle a baseball game by converting it into a spelling lesson, we see that baseball is bizarrely irrelevant to spelling. If we reflect further that a child who is a poor speller might yet be a magnificent ballplayer, we are even further impressed that learning spelling through baseball is learning by absurd association.

In making spelling into a baseball game one drags into the classroom whatever associations a child may have to the impersonal sorting process of kid baseball, but there are differences between the baseball world and the spelling baseball world also. One's failure is paraded before the class minute upon minute, until, when the worst spellers are the only ones left, the conspicuousness of the failures has been enormously increased. Thus the *noise* from baseball is amplified by a *noise* factor specific to the classroom.

It should not be imagined that I "object" to all of this, for in the first place I am aware of the indispensable social functions of the spelling game, and in the second place, I can see that the rendering of failure conspicuous cannot but intensify the quality of the essential nightmare, and thus render an important service to the culture. Without nightmares human culture has never been possible. Without hatred competition cannot take place except in games.

The unremitting effort by the system to bring the cultural drives to a fierce pitch must ultimately turn the children against one another; and though they cannot punch one another in the nose or pull one another's hair in class, they can vent some of their hostility in carping criticism of one another's work. Carping criticism, painfully evident in almost any American classroom, is viciously destructive of the early tillage of those creative impulses we say we cherish.

Listen to a fifth-grade class: The children are taking turns reading stories they have made up. Charlie's is called *The Unknown Guest.*

"One dark, dreary night, on a hill a house stood. This house was forbidden territory for Bill and Joe, but they were going in anyway. The door creaked, squealed, slammed. A voice warned them to go home. They went upstairs. A stair cracked. They entered a room. A voice said they might as well stay and find out now; and their father came out. He laughed and they laughed, but they never forgot their adventure together."

Teacher: Are there any words that give you the mood of the story?

Lucy: He could have made the sentences a little better. . . .

Teacher: Let's come back to Lucy's comment. What about his sentences?

Gert: They were too short. [Charlie and Jeanne have a

discussion about the position of the word "stood" in the first sentence.]

Teacher: Wait a minute; some people are forgetting their manners. . . .

Jeff: About the room: the boys went up the stairs and one "cracked," then they were in the room. Did they fall through the stairs, or what?

[The teacher suggests Charlie make that a little clearer....]

Teacher: We still haven't decided about the short sentences. Perhaps they make the story more spooky and mysterious.

Gwynne: I wish he had read with more expression instead of all at one time.

Rachel: Not enough expression.

Teacher: Charlie, they want a little more expression from you. I guess we've given you enough suggestions for one time. [Charlie does not raise his head, which is bent over his desk as if studying a paper.] Charlie! I guess we've given you enough suggestions for one time, Charlie, haven't we?

If American children fail while one of their number succeeds, they carp. And why not? We must not let our own "inner Borises" befog our thinking. A competitive culture endures by tearing people down. Why blame the children for doing it?

The contemporary school is not all horrors; it has its gentler aspects as well. Nearing a conclusion, let us examine impulse release and affection as they appear in many suburban classrooms.

Impulse is the root of life, and its release in the right amount, time, and place is a primary concern of culture. Nowadays the problem of impulse release takes on a special character because of the epoch's commitment to "letting down the bars." This being the case, teachers have a task unique in the history of education: the fostering of impulse release rather than the installation of controls. Everywhere controls are breaking down, and firmness with impulse is no part of contemporary pedagogy of "the normal child." Rather, impulse release, phrased as "spontaneity," "life adjustment," "democracy," "permissiveness," and "mothering," has become a central doctrine of education. It persists despite tough-minded critics from the Eastern Seaboard who concentrate on curriculum. The teachers know better; the real, the persisting, subject matter is *noise*.

How can the teacher release children's emotions without unchaining chaos? How can she permit so much *noise* and not lose the message? Were they alive, the teachers I had in P.S. 10 and P.S. 186 in New York City, who insisted on absolute silence, would say that chaos does prevail in many modern classrooms and that the message *is* lost. But lest old-fashioned readers argue that the social structure has fallen apart, I will point out what does *not* happen: The children do not fight or wrestle, run around the room, throw things, sing loudly, or whistle. The boys do not attack the girls or vice versa. Children do not run in and out of the room. They do not make the teacher's life miserable. All this occurs when the social structure *is* torn down, but in the average suburban classrooms we studied, it never quite happens. Why not? Here are some excerpts from an interview with a second-grade teacher I'll call Mrs. Olan.

In the one-room schoolhouse in which I first taught, the children came from calm homes. There was no worry about war, and there was no TV or radio. Children of today know more about what is going on; they are better informed. So you can't hold a strict rein on them.

Children need to enjoy school and like it. They also need their work to be done; it's not all play. You must get them to accept responsibility and to do work on their own.

To the question, "What would you say is your own particular way of keeping order in the classroom?" Mrs. Olan says:

Well, I would say I try to get that at the beginning of the year by getting this bond of affection and a relationship between the children and me. And we do that with stories; and I play games *with* them—don't just teach them how to play. It's what you get from living together comfortably. We have "share" times. . . . These are the things that contribute toward discipline. Another thing in discipline—it took me a long time to learn it, too: I thought I was the boss, but I learned that even with a child, if you speak to him as you would to a neighbor or a friend you get a better response than if you say, "Johnny, do this or that."

Mrs. Olan has a creed: Love is the path to discipline through permissiveness; and school is a continuation of family life, in which the values of sharing and democracy lead to comfortable living and ultimately to discipline. She continues:

With primary children the teacher is a mother during the day; they have to be able to bring their problems to you. They get love and affection at home, and I see no reason not to give it in school.

To Mrs. Olan, mother of a 21-year-old son, second-grade children are pussy-cats. When asked, "Do you think the children tend to be quieter if the teacher is affectionate?" she says:

If a teacher has a well-modulated voice and a pleasing disposition, her children are more relaxed and quiet. Children are like kittens: If kittens have a full stomach and lie in the sun they purr. If the atmosphere is such that the children are more comfortable, they are quiet. It is comfortable living that makes the quiet child. When you are shouting at them and they're shouting back at you, it isn't comfortable living.

It is clear to the observer that Mrs. Olan is no "boss," but lodges responsibility in the children. She clarifies the matter further:

It means a great deal to them to give them their own direction. When problems do come up in the room we talk them over and discuss what is the right thing to do when this or that happens. Usually you get pretty good answers. They are a lot harder on themselves than I would be; so if any punishment comes along like not going to an assembly you have group pressure.

As the interviewer was leaving, Mrs. Olan remarked, "My children don't rate as high [on achievement tests] as other children. I don't push, and that's because I believe in comfortable living." *Noise* has indeed become subject matter.

In such classrooms the contemporary training for impulse release and fun is clear. There the children are not in uniform, but in the jerkins and gossamer of *The Midsummer Night's Dream*; it is a sweet drilling without pain. Since impulse and release and fun are a major requirement of the classroom, and since they must be contained within the four walls, the instrument of containment can only be affection. The teacher must therefore become a parent, for it is a parent above all who deals with the impulses of the child.

It is hard for us to see, since we consider most people inherently replaceable, that there is anything remarkable in a parent-figure like a teacher showering the symbols of affection on a child for a year and then letting him walk out of her life. However, this is almost unheard of outside the stream of Western civilization; and even in the West it is not common. As a matter of fact, the existence of *children* willing to accept such demonstrations is in itself an interesting phenomenon, based probably on the obsolescence of the two-parent family. (Today our children *do not have enough parents,* because parents are unable to do all that has to be done *by* parents nowadays.) The fact that a teacher can be demonstrative without inflicting deep wounds on *herself* implies a character structure having strong brakes on involvement. Her expressions of tenderness, then, must imply "so far and no farther"; and over the years, children must come to recognize this. If this were not so, children would have to be dragged shrieking from grade to grade and teachers would flee teaching, for the mutual attachment would be so deep that its annual severing would be too much for either to bear. And so this noise, too, teaches two lessons important to today's culture. From regular replacement-in-affection children learn that the affection-giving figure, the teacher, is replaceable also, and so they are drilled in uninvolvement. Meanwhile, they learn that the symbols of affectivity can be used ambiguously, and that they are not binding—that they can be scattered upon the world without commitment.

Again, the reader should not imagine that I am "against" affectionate classrooms. They are a necessary adjunct to contemporary childhood and to the socialization of parenthood (the "three-parent family") at this stage of our culture. Meanwhile, the dialectic of culture suggests that there is some probability that when love like this enters by the door, learning leaves by the transom.

What, then, is the central issue? The central issue is *love of knowledge* for its own sake, not as the creature of drive, exploited largely for survival and for prestige. Creative cultures have loved the "beautiful person"—meditative, intellectual, and exalted. As for the individual, the history of great civilizations reveals little except that creativity has had an obstinate way of emerging only in a few, and that it has never appeared in the mass of the people. Loving the beautiful person more, we may alter this.

The contemporary school is a place where children are drilled in very general cultural orientations, and where subject matter becomes to a very considerable extent the instrument for instilling them. Because school deals with masses of children, it can manage only by reducing children all to a common definition. Naturally that definition is determined by the cultural preoccupations and so school creates the *essential nightmare* that drives people away from something (in our case, failure) and toward something (success). Today our children, instead of loving knowledge, become embroiled in the nightmare.

Directions for Essay 7

Return to your incident at school in essay 5—or select and describe a new incident if you prefer. Then analyze, rewrite, resee this experience in relation to some of Jules Henry's terms, such as noise, nightmare, dream of failure, love of knowledge.

I have tried to give my picture of the characteristic attributes of the person who emerges; a person who is more open to all the elements of his organic experience; a person who is learning to live in his life as a participant in a fluid, ongoing process, in which he is continually discovering new aspects of himself in the flow of his experience.

CARL R. ROGERS

Chapter
8
Education
as Awareness

In 1971, a teacher at Yale named Charles A. Reich created a stir with a book called *The Greening of America*. In it he argued for the virtues of the young, the liberated, the "now generation." The attitudes of this generation—*your* generation?—he subsumed under the title "Consciousness III," a consciousness that seeks to preserve the individual self in the face of organized government, organized technology, organized old folks. You can sense something of the point of view, as well as Mr. Reich's style, from the following paragraph:

In light of what we have said, we can now see the true significance of the central fact about Consciousness III—its assertion of the power to *choose* a way of life. The people who came to this country chose a life-style; it was for that freedom of choice that they left their native countries. But when the machine took over, men lost the power of choice, and their lives were molded to fit the domination of the machine. The

machine slavery, extending upward to the white collar and
professional ranks, became the key reality of twentieth-century
existence. The power of choice, the power to transcend, is
exactly what has been missing in America for so long. That is
why a new life-style is capable of dismantling the Corporate
State, when both liberal reform and radical tactics are
powerless. The elements of that life may vary and change; the
supreme act is the act of choice. For the choice of a life-style is
an act of transcendence of the machine, an act of independence, a declaration of independence. We are entering a new
age of man.*

To conclude our series that began with chapter 5—seeing
yourself as student—we are going to look at Reich's remarks on
education in the light of Consciousness III. As you read the
following pages, be alert to the way that word, education, is
being redefined. And be alert too, of course, to ways in which
you might resee your own experience, "educational" or not, in
these new terms.

Education and Consciousness III
CHARLES A. REICH

The first major theme of this new way of life must
be education—education not in the limited sense of training in
school, but in its largest and most humanistic meaning. The
central American problem might be defined as a failure of
education. We have vastly underestimated the amount of
education and consciousness that is required to meet the

* *The Greening of America*, p. 354.

From *The Greening of America*. Copyright © 1970 by Charles A. Reich.
Reprinted by permission of Random House, Inc. Originally appeared in *The
New Yorker* in somewhat different form.

demands of organization and technology. Most of our "education" has taught us how to *operate* the technology; how to
function as a human component of an organization. What we
need is education that will enable us to make use of
technology, control it and give it direction, cause it to serve
values which we have chosen.

We have already shown, in discussing the industrializa-
tion of America and the New Deal, that Americans never
faced the question of how much education and understanding
would be necessary if mass democracy were really to be
effective in a technological society. Even before technology, de
Tocqueville and others expressed well-justified skepticism
about self-government by poorly educated masses. The New
Deal tried to rely on experts and specialists, but quite aside
from their own failings, they could not govern an electorate
that did not understand. Our failure in democracy has now
been surpassed by our failure in control of the things we have
made, and our even greater failure to realize the affirmative
possibilities of technology. We know how to drive a car, but we
do not know how to keep cars from destroying our environment, or how to use a car to make cities and countryside more
beautiful and more of a community, and to make man's life
more creative and liberated. Henry James was acutely aware
of this incapacity; he believed that time, tradition, and
sensibility were needed to "civilize" manufactured innovation.
We can give his ideas a contemporary meaning by saying that
today education and consciousness are needed to humanize all
the new forms of work, things, and experiences that are thrust
upon us.

We are prone to think of the capacity to make affirmative
use of innovations as a moral quality, an aspect of "character."
A man who drives to the country for a picnic, drowns out the
sounds of nature with a transistor radio, and leaves beer cans
strewn around when he departs is said to lack "character."
This is the same fallacy of the human heart that has made us
see so many issues of government and technology as moral

questions. Capacity to appreciate nature, to benefit from it, and to be enhanced by it is a matter of education. The beauty and fascination of nature is not available to the uneducated eye, any more than the beauty of painting or poetry. But it is not just a question of specific education, it is a question of a more general consciousness, a readiness to receive new experiences in a certain way.

We have also greatly underestimated the amount and kind of education needed to make any given individual able to adapt to change. The individual whose education stops at eighteen or twenty-one is a pathetic sight in our society. Increasingly he is obsolete in his work; he is kept on because of his long service, and would be unable to find a new job if he lost his existing one. He is unable to understand his society, unable to vote in a responsible way, unable to communicate with his own children, or to understand their culture. He is allowed to become human wreckage, because his mind stopped growing while all the elements around him moved on ahead.

Our present ideas of education are absurdly narrow and primitive for the kinds of tasks men face; education now is little more than training for the industrial army. What is needed is just the opposite of what we now have. A person should question what he is told and what he reads. He should demand the basis upon which experts or authorities have reached a conclusion. He should doubt his own teachers. He should believe that his own subjective feelings are of value. He should make connections and see relationships where the attempt has been made to keep them separate. He should appreciate the diversity of things and ideas rather than be told that one particular way is the "right" way. He should be exposed and re-exposed to as wide a variety of experience and contrasts as possible. Above all, he should learn to search for and develop his own potential, his own individuality, his own uniqueness. That is what the word "educate" literally means. What we urgently need is not training but education, not indoctrination but the expansion of each individual—a process continuing throughout life; in a word, education for consciousness.

Such education cannot stop at the age of twenty-one. We now "educate" most of our people through high school, a minority through college, and virtually nobody thereafter. When a difficult choice comes along, such as whether the noise of the SST is worth its additional speed in crossing the country, the thinking of most of the population over thirty turns out to have frozen as of the time their education ceased, so that they think that our greatest need is "advances" in technology. Thus, even if "education" itself were adequate, a majority of the people would no longer be learning or thinking. Dr. Kenneth Keniston has said that youth is emerging as a new and separate stage of life—a time for gaining experience and learning, for acquiring consciousness, we might say. Dr. Keniston seems to be correct in this, but the stage of life that he calls "youth" is better described as the stage of education. "Youth" in this sense must now of necessity continue all through life.

In the light of these needs, we can place much of the culture and attitudes of the new generation in perspective; we can see that the new generation has been attempting to develop its own form of education along the lines we have described. Much of what seems to outsiders to be aimless or self-indulgent turns out, when reexamined, to fit precisely the true requirements for education today. Activities which seem irrational all make perfect sense as part of a higher reason; they are good for the individual and good for society.

The new generation insists upon being open to all experience. It will experiment with anything, even though the new "trip" does not fit into any preconceived notion of the individual's personality. If a Consciousness II person, old or young, is asked whether he wants to see a far-out film, try a new drug, or spend a week living in a nature-food commune, he feels uncomfortable and refuses; the experiment is out of keeping with his already established character. The new consciousness is always flexible, curious, and ready to add something new to his "character." At the same time, the new generation constantly tries to break away from the older, established forms which, in a changing society, must forever be obsolete. Authority, schedules, time, accepted customs, are all forms which must be questioned. Accepted patterns of thought must be broken; what is considered "rational thought" must be opposed by "nonrational thought"—drug-thought, mysticism, impulses. Of course the latter kinds of thought are not really "nonrational" at all; they merely introduce new elements into the sterile, rigid, outworn "rationality" that prevails today.

Young people today insist upon prolonging the period of youth, education, and growth. They stay uncommitted; they refuse to decide on a formal career, they do not give themselves fixed future goals to pursue. Their emphasis on the present makes possible an openness toward the future; the person who focusses on the future freezes that future in its present image. Personal relationships are entered into without commitment to the future; a marriage legally binding for the life of the couple is inconsistent with the likelihood of growth and change; if the couple grows naturally together that is fine, but change, not an unchanging love, is the rule of life.

Seeking an education for an unknowable future, the new generation rejects the idea that a school or college is the only possible institution to supply it. The new consciousness uses many other "institutions" for its education. It founds "free schools" as alternatives to high schools or colleges. It seeks job-experiences such as work in a ghetto school, or migrant labor, or the Peace Corps. It takes part in political activism and radical politics with education in mind. It uses underground newspapers, work in theatre or film, summers in the wilderness, or a rock festival, as institutions of education. Just as an earlier school of hard knocks gave the frontiersman his practicality and adaptability, so today's efforts to transcend the terms of society make possible an open consciousness for a frontier far more unknown than that of the pioneers. . . .

A fundamental object of the education we have described is transcendence, or personal liberation. It is a liberation that is both personal and communal, an escape from the limits fixed by custom and society, in pursuit of something better and higher. It is epitomized in the concept of "choosing a life-style"; the idea that an individual need not accept the pattern that society has formed for him, but may make his own choice. It is seen visually in the growth of the student-gypsy world, a new geography of hitchhikers, knapsacks, sleeping bags, and the open road: not a summer vacation or a journey from one fixed point to another, but a new sense of existence in the immediate present, without fixed points. It can be heard in the song from the rock opera "Tommy" by the Who, "I'm Free."

To talk about transcendence in a less metaphorical way, we might consider the thinking behind the creation of People's Park in Berkeley. There was a large, muddy lot near the campus in Berkeley. It was the property of the University of California, which expected to make use of it for university purposes in due time. But a group of people, "street people" and students, thought it should be used for a park. They saw it in terms of the human and ecological situation of the city. They utterly failed or refused to see it in legal terms, as "private property." In placing human needs and ecology (as they saw them) ahead of "law," they proposed nothing less than a new social order. They proposed a society in which aesthetics, ecology, and human requirements would be paramount, and in which decisions concerning these matters would be made not by the persons designated by law in our society, but by self-constituted local groups whose legitimacy came only from their proximity and concern. To call this "anarchy" is to miss the point. It was not anarchy but a wholly different form of society, with different priorities, different sources of authority, a different process of decision-making. Perhaps the new form was not a viable or desirable one. But by their actions, the makers of People's Park hoped to further our liberation from the current forms of society, so that we might be free to choose among new forms of social order, just as individuals might be free to choose among life-styles. Social forms, the creators of People's Park might say, are not absolutes, they are mere machinery. Like any other machinery, it cannot supply man with a view of what life should be. It cannot take from him the responsibility for answering that question. Reason does not begin or end with any form of government. Liberation means freedom to search for the highest form of man's existence.

The creative, imaginative, life-giving power of transcendence can be seen whenever Consciousness III people are found. They transform a city rooftop in Berkeley into a theatre for watching the sunset and the lighting of the darkened city. They transform the impersonal toll booth plazas of the Massachusetts Turnpike and the New York Thruway into something interesting, comical, and filled with possibilities for meeting new people. They make the sidewalk into a place for sitting, and the night a time for staying up. They place a sculpture of a giant lipstick in the middle of a pompous plaza, and bring sterility back to life. They are the genii of change and transmutation, and thus they fulfill the ultimate biological need to change, to adapt, to grow, to die, and to be reborn.

The concept of education we have used up to now, although far broader than formal "education," is still not adequate to our meaning. For we are really speaking of the continuing growth of awareness and consciousness, the search for new dimensions of experience. It is this undertaking that Ken Kesey pursued as Tom Wolfe describes it in *The Electric Kool-Aid Acid Test*—not a frolic, but a purposeful undertaking using drugs, costumes, day-glo paint, a cross-country trip in a psychedelic bus, the founding of a Pranksters' community in California, a series of "fantasies" played out with the Hell's Angels, the Unitarians, the Acid Tests, and finally the Acid

Test graduation—an undertaking that represented a serious search for awareness and new knowledge. It is the same search for awareness that might make one drive 100 miles and then turn around and come home, or travel to the beach or mountains, or look upon any experience—a laundromat on Telegraph Avenue in Berkeley, a lunch at a businessman's seafood restaurant in downtown San Francisco, a lawyer's conference in Washington, D.C., a visit to an ice cream parlor in Seattle—as a "trip" to some new dimension. The attitude of Kesey, like that of Henry James or Wallace Stevens, placed a supreme value on the development of consciousness, sensitivity, experience, knowledge. No trouble, no expense, no disruption, no uprooting, could stand in the way of the continuing growth of one's mind.

The task in composing essay 8 is to see yourself once more as student, but this time through the eyes of Consciousness III. You don't have to agree with Reich's values; in fact you can make your essay a criticism of his point of view if you wish. The object is to try applying, sympathetically or not, some of Reich's terms and definitions to your own case.

Notice how Reich defines by redefining. That is, he repeatedly argues that what *seems* (to old fogeys) non-educational or frivolous, is "really" educational in his sense of the word. Here is an example (page 122): "Much of what seems to outsiders to be aimless or self-indulgent turns out, when reexamined, to fit precisely the true requirements for education today. Activities which seem irrational all make perfect sense as part of a higher reason; they are good for the individual and good for society." Here, activities that some people name as aimless, self-indulgent, irrational are redefined by Reich as "part of a higher reason." A fair question is, what sort of activities? And is "high reason" more than just an elegant and honorific phrase? These could be questions for you to answer in your essay from your own point of view.

You could for example choose an experience of yours that

might fall under the categories of "drug-thought, mysticism, impulses" (page 123). Such experiences, says the author, "are not really 'nonrational' at all; they merely introduce new elements into the sterile, rigid, outworn 'rationality' that prevails today." Has this been true for you? Can you identify in your own life some "new elements" that have helped you to resist sterility and rigidity?

To take another example (page 124), if you have yourself engaged in the "student-gypsy world," "on the road" for a period of time, can you speak of it as education in Reich's sense? Can you persuade a reader that you had "a new sense of existence in the immediate present"?

And still another example: reread the paragraph on the People's Park in Berkeley. Notice how the conflict can be viewed as a war over definitions. Where authorities used terms like law and private property, the street people spoke of human requirements and new priorities. One man's "anarchy" is another man's "new social order." Here is another emergence of our old friend *ambiguity*. Have you had educational experiences that could be seen in this way, as a conflict between values expressed in contrasting labels?

Directions for Essay 8

See an experience of yours as "educational" in Reich's terms. (In the process, you can support or attack Reich's premises, as you wish.) See your experience—in class or out, stoned, on the road, or whatever—as potentially contributing to "growth of awareness and consciousness." Be as precise as you can in answering the questions, awareness of what? Consciousness of what?

The truth must be
*That you do not see, you experience, you
feel,*
*That the buxom eye brings merely its ele-
ment*
*To the total thing, a shapeless giant forced
Upward.*
Green were the curls upon that head.
WALLACE STEVENS*

Chapter
9
Seeing
a Church Façade

With
chapter 9 we return to a problem of immediate visual seeing.
How do you see a building? How do you see (for instance) the
front of a church? Here we face some familiar difficulties which
by now you ought to be able to approach with some confidence. What about point of view? All senses of this phrase are
important. To describe the front of a church you will need a
particular physical *point* to begin with, from which your steps
or your moving eyes can carry your reader to various aspects of
the church façade. These movements must, of course, be
orderly. For example, one might begin with a general impression, as from a distance; then, approaching closer, one might let
one's eyes travel from bottom to top, or from top to bottom. In
any case the reader must have an impression that he is being
led to see this building in a fashion that has some connection

* From "Poem Written at Morning" from *The Collected Poems of
Wallace Stevens* by permission of the publisher, Alfred A. Knopf, Inc.
Copyright 1942, 1954 by Wallace Stevens.

with an actual experience of looking. But point of view in its other senses of attitude and tone of voice are, of course, important here too. Who are you, who should you be, as you speak to a reader about the appearance of a church?

The reading matter this time is inspirational—that is, the author is a man who elegantly handles all these problems, for your edification and delight. He is the great novelist Henry James, and he is taking us to a great church, the Cathedral of Notre-Dame at Chartres, a short distance from Paris. As you will see, he is in no hurry.

Chartres

HENRY JAMES

The spring, in Paris, since it has fairly begun, has been enchanting. The sun and the moon have been blazing in emulation, and the difference between the blue sky of day and of night has been as slight as possible. There are no clouds in the sky, but there are little thin green clouds, little puffs of raw, tender verdure, entangled among the branches of the trees. All the world is in the street; the chairs and tables which have stood empty all winter before the doors of the cafés are at a premium; the theatres have become intolerably close; the puppet-shows in the Champs Élysées are the only form of dramatic entertainment which seems consistent with the season. By way of doing honour, at a small cost, to this

From *Portraits of Places* (Boston: James R. Osgood & Co., 1884), copyright 1883 by James R. Osgood & Co. This essay was revised by James from a travel-letter he published originally in the New York *Tribune* in April, 1876. The original version has been reprinted elsewhere, in Henry James's *Parisian Sketches*, eds. Leon Edel and Ilse Dusoir Lind (New York: New York University Press, 1957).

ethereal mildness, I went out the other day to the ancient town of Chartres, where I spent several hours, which I cannot consent to pass over as if nothing had happened. It is the experience of the writer of these lines, who likes nothing so much as moving about to see the world, that if one has been for a longer time than usual resident and stationary, there is a kind of overgrown entertainment in taking the train, even for a suburban goal; and that if one takes it on a charming April day, when there is a sense, almost an odour, of change in the air, the innocent pleasure is as nearly as possible complete. My accessibility to emotions of this kind amounts to an infirmity, and the effect of it was to send me down to Chartres in a shamelessly optimistic state of mind. I was so prepared to be entertained and pleased with everything that it is only a mercy that the cathedral happens really to be a fine building. If it had not been, I should still have admired it inordinately, at the risk of falling into heaven knows what aesthetic heresy. But I am almost ashamed to say how soon my entertainment began. It began, I think, with my hailing a little open carriage on the boulevard and causing myself to be driven to the Gare de l'Ouest—far away across the river, up the Rue Bonaparte, of art-student memories, and along the big, straight Rue de Rennes to the Boulevard Montparnasse. Of course, at this rate, by the time I reached Chartres—the journey is of a couple of hours—I had almost drained the cup of pleasure. But it was replenished at the station, at the buffet, from the pungent bottle of wine I drank with my breakfast. Here, by the way, is another excellent excuse for being delighted with any day's excursion in France—that wherever you are, you may breakfast to your taste. There may, indeed, if the station is very small, be no buffet; but if there is a buffet, you may be sure that civilisation—in the persons of a sympathetic young woman in a well-made black dress, and a rapid, zealous, grateful waiter—presides at it. It was quite the least, as the French say, that after my breakfast I should have thought the cathedral, as I saw it from the top of the steep hill on which the town stands, rising high above the clustered houses, and seeming to make of their red-roofed agglomeration a mere pedestal for its immense beauty, promised remarkably well. You see it so as you emerge from the station, and then, as you climb slowly into town, you lose sight of it. You perceive empty open *places*, and crooked shady streets, in which two or three times you lose your way, until at last, after more than once catching a glimpse, high above some slit between the houses, of the clear gray towers shining against the blue sky, you push forward again, risk another short cut, turn another interposing corner, and stand before the goal of your pilgrimage.

I spent a long time looking at this monument. I revolved around it, like a moth around a candle; I went away and I came back; I chose twenty different standpoints; I observed it during the different hours of the day, and saw it in the moonlight as well as the sunshine. I gained, in a word, a certain sense of familiarity with it; and yet I despair of giving any coherent account of it. Like most French cathedrals, it rises straight out of the street, and is destitute of that setting of turf and trees and deaneries and canonries which contribute so largely to the impressiveness of the great English churches. Thirty years ago a row of old houses was glued to its base and made their back walls of its sculptured sides. These have been plucked away, and, relatively speaking, the church is fairly isolated. But the little square that surrounds it is deplorably narrow, and you flatten your back against the opposite houses in the vain attempt to stand off and survey the towers. The proper way to look at them would be to go up in a balloon and hang poised, face to face with them, in the blue air. There is, however, perhaps an advantage in being forced to stand so directly under them, for this position gives you an overwhelming impression of their height. I have seen, I suppose, churches as beautiful as this one, but I do not remember ever to have been so fascinated by superpositions and vertical effects. The endless upward reach of the great west front, the clear, silvery tone of its surface, the way three or four magnificent features are made to occupy its serene expanse, its simplicity, majesty, and dignity—these things crowd upon one's sense with a force that makes the act of vision seem for the moment almost all of life. The impressions produced by architecture lend themselves as little to interpretation by another medium as those produced by music. Certainly there is an inexpressible harmony in the façade of Chartres.

The doors are rather low, as those of the English cathedrals are apt to be, but (standing three together) are set in a deep framework of sculpture—rows of arching grooves, filled with admirable little images, standing with their heels on each other's heads. The church, as it now exists, except the northern tower, dates from the middle of the thirteenth century, and these closely packed figures are full of the grotesqueness of the period. Above the triple portals is a vast round-topped window, in three divisions, of the grandest dimensions and the stateliest effect. Above this window is a circular aperture, of huge circumference, with a double row of sculptured spokes radiating from its centre and looking on its lofty field of stone as expansive and symbolic as if it were the wheel of Time itself. Higher still is a little gallery with a delicate balustrade, supported on a beautiful cornice and stretching across the front from tower to tower; and above this is a range of niched statues of kings—fifteen, I believe, in number. Above the statues is a gable, with an image of the Virgin and Child on its front, and another of Christ on its apex. In the relation of all these parts there is such a high felicity that while on the one side the eye rests on a great many large blanks there is no approach on the other to poverty. The little gallery that I have spoken of, beneath the statues of the kings, had for me a peculiar charm. Useless, at its tremendous altitude, for other purposes, it seemed intended for the little images to step down and walk about upon. When the great façade begins to glow in the late afternoon light, you can imagine them strolling up and down their long balcony in couples, pausing with their elbows on the balustrade, resting their stony chins in their hands, and looking out, with their little blank eyes, on the great view of the old French monarchy they once ruled, and which now has passed away. The two great towers of the cathedral are among the noblest of their kind. They rise in solid simplicity to a height as great as the eye often troubles itself to travel, and then suddenly they begin to execute a magnificent series of feats in architectural gymnastics. This is especially true of the northern spire, which is a late creation, dating from the sixteenth century. The other is relatively quiet; but its companion is a sort of tapering bouquet of sculptured stone. Statues and buttresses, gargoyles, arabesques and crockets pile themselves in successive stages, until the eye loses the sense of everything but a sort of architectural lacework. The pride of Chartres, after its front, is the two portals of its transepts—great dusky porches, in three divisions, covered with more images than I have time to talk about. Wherever you look, along the sides of the church, a time-worn image is niched or perched. The face of each flying buttress is garnished with one, with the features quite melted away.

The inside of the cathedral corresponds in vastness and grandeur to the outside—it is the perfection of gothic in its prime. But I looked at it rapidly, the place was so intolerably cold. It seemed to answer one's query of what becomes of the winter when the spring chases it away. The winter hereabouts has sought an asylum in Chartres cathedral, where it has found plenty of room and may reside in a state of excellent preservation until it can safely venture abroad again. I supposed I had been in cold churches before, but the delusion had been an injustice to the temperature of Chartres. The nave was full of the little padded chairs of the local bourgeoisie, whose faith, I hope for their comfort, is of good old red-hot complexion. In a higher temperature I should have done more justice to the magnificent old glass of the windows—which glowed through the icy dusk like the purple and orange of a winter sunset—and to the immense sculptured external casing of the choir. This latter is an extraordinary piece of work. It is a high gothic screen, shutting in the choir, and covered with elaborate bas-reliefs of the sixteenth and seventeenth centuries, representing scenes from the life of Christ and of the Virgin. Some of the figures are admirable, and the effect of the whole great semicircular wall, chiselled like a silver bowl, is superb. There is also a crypt of high antiquity, and, I believe, great interest, to be seen; but my teeth chattered a respectful negative to the sacristan who offered to guide me to it. It was so agreeable to stand in the warm outer air again, that I spent the rest of the day in it.

Although, besides its cathedral, Chartres has no very rare architectural treasures, the place is pictorial, in a shabby, third-rate, poverty-stricken degree, and my observations were not unremunerative. There is a little church of Saint-Aignan, of the sixteenth century, with an elegant, decayed facade, and a small tower beside it, lower than its own roof, to which it is joined, in unequal twinship, by a single long buttress. Standing there with its crumbling Renaissance doorway, in a kind of grass-grown alcove, it reminded me of certain monuments that the tourist encounters in small Italian towns. Most of the streets of Chartres are crooked lanes, winding over the face of the steep hill, the summit of the hill being occupied by half a dozen little open squares, which seem like reservoirs of the dulness and stillness that flow through the place. In the midst of one of them rises an old dirty brick obelisk, commemorating the glories of the young General Marceau, of the first Republic—"Soldier at 16, general at 23, he died at 27." Such memorials, when one comes upon them unexpectedly, produce in the mind a series of circular waves of feeling, like a splash in a quiet pond. Chartres gives us an impression of extreme antiquity, but it is an antiquity that has gone down in the world. I saw very few of those stately little hôtels, with pilastered fronts, which look so well in the silent streets of provincial towns. The houses are mostly low, small, and of sordid aspect, and though many of them have overhanging upper stories, and steep, battered gables, they are rather wanting in character. I was struck, as an American always is in small French and English towns, with the immense number of shops, and their brilliant appearance, which seems so out of proportion to any visible body of consumers. At Chartres the shopkeepers must all feed upon each other, for, whoever buys, the whole population sells. This population appeared to consist mainly of several hundred brown old peasant women, in the seventies and eighties, with their faces cross-hatched with wrinkles and their quaint white coifs drawn tightly over their weather-blasted eye-brows. Labour-stricken grandams, all the world over, are the opposite of lovely, for the toil that wrestles for its daily bread, morsel by morsel, is not beautifying; but I thought I had never seen the possibilities of female ugliness so variously embodied as in the crones of Chartres. Some of them were leading small children by the hand—little red-cheeked girls, in the close black caps and black pinafores of humble French infancy—a costume which makes French children always look like orphans. Others were guiding along the flinty lanes the steps of small donkeys, some of them fastened into little carts, some with well-laden backs. These were the only quadrupeds I perceived at Chartres. Neither horse nor carriage did I behold, save at the station the omnibuses of the rival inns—the "Grand Monarque" and the "Duc de Chartres"—which glare at each other across the Grande Place. A friend of mine told me that a few years ago, passing through Chartres, he went by night to call upon a gentleman who lived there. During his visit it came on to rain violently, and when the hour for his departure arrived the rain had made the streets impassable. There was no vehicle to be had, and my friend was resigning himself to a soaking. "You can be taken of course in the sedan-chair," said his host with dignity. The sedan-chair was produced, a couple of serving-men grasped the handles, my friend stepped into it, and went swinging back—through the last century—to the "Grand

Monarque." This little anecdote, I imagine, still paints Chartres socially.

Before dinner I took a walk on the planted promenade which encircles the town—the Tour-de-ville it is called— much of which is extremely picturesque. Chartres has lost her walls as a whole, but here and there they survive, and play a desultory part in holding the town together. In one place the rampart is really magnificent—smooth, strong and lofty, curtained with ivy, and supporting on its summit an old convent and its garden. Only one of the city-gates remains—a narrow arch of the fourteenth century, flanked by two admirable round towers, and preceded by a fosse. If you stoop a little, as you stand outside, the arch of this hoary old gate makes a capital setting for the picture of the interior of the town, and, on the inner hill-top, against the sky, the large gray mass of the Cathedral. The ditch is full, and to right and to the left it flows along the base of the mouldering wall, through which the shabby backs of houses extrude, and which is garnished with little wooden galleries, lavatories of the town's soiled linen. These little galleries are filled with washerwomen, who crane over and dip their many-colored rags into the yellow stream. The old patched and interrupted wall, the ditch with its weedy edges, the spots of color, the white-capped laundresses in their little wooden cages—one lingers to look at it all.

The two paragraphs in which James actually encounters the façade of Chartres and tries to come to terms with it begin on page 131, and we might pause over this encounter to admire the way he does it.

The *point* from which James attempts to *view* the façade is complicated, and indeed its complication is in part his subject. He is playful, as well as eager and enthusiastic, as he approaches his point, in a physical sense, by walking through the crooked streets of Chartres, and his use of the second person forces a kind of sharing on the part of the reader. "You push forward again, risk another short cut, turn another interposing corner, and stand before the goal of your pilgrimage."

So here we are at last: the monument. Now James engages in a series of half-ludicrous backings and fillings, trying quite self-consciously to find a point of view where he can settle. "I revolved around it, like a moth around a candle; I went away and I came back; I chose twenty different standpoints." But the scene is too much. "I despair of giving any coherent account of it." (Does he really despair? What does he, what does he not, despair of?) Part of his problem of finding a place to stand, as he says in the next few sentences, is due to the general structure of the square, where "you flatten your back against the opposite houses in the vain attempt to stand off and survey the towers." Maybe a balloon would do it! But a truer cause of these difficulties is to be found in the inexpressible quality of the façade itself, as James indicates in the remainder of the paragraph: "endless upward reach," "clear, silvery tone," "simplicity, majesty, dignity." These abstractions imply by their very vagueness the difficulties the speaker is suffering in communication. Physically he has not been able to find a place to stand, but in any case, as a man working with words, he finds himself confronting a "vision" that is simply not translatable into language. The subject of this paragraph might be defined as the problem of finding a point of view and translating experience into words, and that problem ought to sound familiar to the student of these exercises. "There is an inexpressible harmony in the façade of Chartres." There is something inexpressible in *any* harmony.

But now to business, and the next paragraph beginning, "The doors are rather low." Granting all these difficulties, James seems to say, let us in our pedestrian way do what we can to describe what we see in the Chartres façade. (You should follow his progress on the photograph, as well as in the paragraph itself.) He begins with the doors, then, and his general route is upward: framework of sculpture around and above the doors, the "vast, round-topped window" above that, the rose window, the balustrade, the statues of kings, and the gable on top. After a flight of fancy about the kings strolling on the balcony, he proceeds upward to the towers, where words again begin to fail. The "architectural gymnastics" of the north tower can be described only in lists of nouns like gargoyles and arabesques, "until the eye loses the sense of everything but a sort of architectural lacework." And he changes the subject, to the transepts.

An important function of this style is its repeated reminder that no style can adequately control such experience. The speaker protests his incapacity throughout, and finally, like any tourist, he turns away with some relief to the shabby town, the touching obelisk, and his dinner.

The problem for you, the student writer, is of course not to sound like Henry James (which has been tried), but to see your own church with your own sensibility and your own style.

Directions for Essay 9

Find a church in your neighborhood that seems to you an interesting building. Describe what you see on its façade in detail, and in such a style that your reader sees it as an interesting building too.

Nothing in education is so astonishing as the amount of ignorance it accumulates in the form of inert facts.

HENRY ADAMS

Chapter
10
The Façade
as History

There are plenty of other points of view from which one might see a church façade. There are other terms available, in addition to those of the modestly elegant observer whose language we admired in chapter 9. An engineer could see the façade in terms of stresses and construction materials; an atheist could call it pablum for the masses; an artist could admire that "glow in the late afternoon light" and reach for his chrome yellow. This list could be protracted. The terms you are about to encounter, however, are those of a historian. The problem in this essay is to determine, so far as one sparkling example can help, how a historian uses his particular language to talk about the façade of Chartres Cathedral, and how you might do likewise with your own church.

You might want to point out that there are some places in the essay by Henry James (who was no historian) where historical statements are made. For instance, James calls the northern tower "a late creation, dating from the sixteenth

Chartres. The two tall spires and the Royal Portal in the main façade form one of the finest groupings in French religious art.

century." Isn't this as historical a remark as one could want? Maybe it is, but you might ask yourself whether such a statement might not also, perfectly appropriately, appear in a guidebook, a piece of tourist talk. Yet as students of the liberal arts, we apparently assume that a historian's way of writing is in some way really different from tourist writing. What is that difference? Is it possible that the mere assigning of a *date* to an event or an object is only the beginning of the historian's task? If so, then what does the rest of his task consist of?

We can begin to suggest some answers to these questions if we read carefully the following piece of historical writing by a recognized historian. Henry Adams, who was a contemporary of Henry James, wrote this description of the towers as part of a famous historical study of the middle ages, *Mont-Saint-Michel and Chartres.* It is not easy reading; there are plenty of names and references you will have to look up in a good encyclopedia. You should also, as you follow Adams' descriptions, refer constantly to the photograph of the cathedral, making sure you can identify the various architectural details that Adams mentions.

The Towers of Chartres

HENRY ADAMS

For a first visit to Chartres, choose some pleasant morning when the lights are soft, for one wants to be welcome, and the cathedral has moods, at times severe. At best, the Beauce is a country none too gay.

The first glimpse that is caught, and the first that was

From *Mont-Saint-Michel and Chartres*, copyright, 1905, by Henry Adams, and 1933, by Charles Francis Adams. Reprinted by permission of Houghton Mifflin Company.

meant to be caught, is that of the two spires. With all the education that Normandy and the Île de France can give, one is still ignorant. The spire is the simplest part of the Romanesque or Gothic architecture, and needs least study in order to be felt. It is a bit of sentiment almost pure of practical purpose. It tells the whole of its story at a glance, and its story is the best that architecture had to tell, for it typified the aspirations of man at the moment when man's aspirations were highest. Yet nine persons out of ten—perhaps ninety-nine in a hundred—who come within sight of the two spires of Chartres will think it a jest if they are told that the smaller of the two, the simpler, the one that impresses them least, is the one which they are expected to recognize as the most perfect piece of architecture in the world. Perhaps the French critics might deny that they make any such absolute claim; in that case you can ask them what their exact claim is; it will always be high enough to astonish the tourist.

Astonished or not, we have got to take this southern spire of the Chartres Cathedral as the object of serious study, and before taking it as art, must take it as history. The foundations of this tower—always to be known as the "old tower"—are supposed to have been laid in 1091, before the first crusade. The flèche was probably half a century later (1145–70). The foundations of the new tower, opposite, were laid not before 1110, when also the portal, which stands between them, was begun with the three lancet windows above it, but not the rose. For convenience, this old façade—including the portal and the two towers, but not the flèches, and the three lancet windows, but not the rose—may be dated as complete about 1150.

Originally the whole portal—the three doors and the three lancets—stood nearly forty feet back, on the line of the interior foundations, or rear wall of the towers. This arrangement threw the towers forward, free on three sides, as at Poitiers, and gave room for a parvis, before the portal—a porch, roofed over, to protect the pilgrims who always stopped there to pray before entering the church. When the church was rebuilt after the great fire of 1194, and the architect was required to enlarge the interior, the old portal and lancets were moved bodily forward, to be flush with the front walls of the two towers, as you see the façade today; and the façade itself was heightened, to give room for the rose, and to cover the loftier pignon and vaulting behind. Finally, the wooden roof, above the stone vault, was masked by the Arcade of Kings and its railing, completed in the taste of Philip the Hardy, who reigned from 1270 to 1285.

These changes have, of course, altered the values of all the parts. The portal is injured by being thrown into a glare of light, when it was intended to stand in shadow, as you will see in the north and south porches over the transept portals. The towers are hurt by losing relief and shadow; but the old flèche is obliged to suffer the cruellest wrong of all by having its right shoulder hunched up by half of a huge rose and the whole of a row of kings, when it was built to stand free, and to soar above the whole façade from the top of its second storey. One can easily figure it so and replace the lost parts of the old façade, more or less at haphazard, from the front of Noyon.

What an outrage it was you can see by a single glance at the new flèche opposite. The architect of 1500 has flatly refused to submit to such conditions, and has insisted, with very proper self-respect, on starting from the balustrade of the Arcade of Kings as his level. Not even content with that, he has carried up his square tower another lofty storey before he would consent to touch the heart of his problem, the conversion of the square tower into the octagon flèche. In doing this, he has sacrificed once more the old flèche; but his own tower stands free as it should.

At Vendôme, when you go there, you will be in a way to appreciate still better what happened to the Chartres flèche; for the clocher at Vendôme, which is of the same date—Viollet-le-Duc says earlier, and Enlart, "after 1130"—stood and still stands free, like an Italian campanile, which gives it a vast advantage. The tower of Saint-Leu-d'Esserent, also after 1130, stands free, above the second storey. Indeed, you will hardly find, in the long list of famous French spires, another which has been treated with so much indignity as this, the greatest and most famous of all; and perhaps the most annoying part of it is that you must be grateful to the architect of 1195 for doing no worse. He has, on the contrary, done his best to show respect for the work of his predecessor, and has done so well that, handicapped as it is, the old tower still defies rivalry. Nearly three hundred and fifty feet high, or, to be exact, 106.5 metres from the church floor, it is built up with an amount of intelligence and refinement that leaves to unprofessional visitors no chance to think a criticism—much less to express one. Perhaps—when we have seen more—and feel less—who knows?—but certainly not now!

"The greatest and surely the most beautiful monument of this kind that we possess in France," says Viollet-le-Duc; but although an ignorant spectator must accept the architect's decision on a point of relative merit, no one is compelled to accept his reasons, as final. "There is no need to dwell," he continues, "upon the beauty and the grandeur of composition in which the artist has given proof of rare sobriety, where all the effects are obtained, not by ornaments, but by the just and skilful proportion of the different parts. The transition, so hard to adjust, between the square base and the octagon of the flèche, is managed and carried out with an address which has not been surpassed in similar monuments." One stumbles a little at the word "adresse." One never caught one's self using the word in Norman churches. Your photographs of Bayeux or Boscherville or Secqueville will show you at a glance whether the term "adresse" applies to them. Even Vendôme would rather be praised for "droiture" than for "adresse."—Whether the word "adresse" means cleverness, dexterity, adroitness, or simple technical skill, the thing itself is something which the French have always admired more than the Normans ever did. Viollet-le-Duc himself seems to be a little uncertain whether to lay most stress on the one or the other quality: "If one tries to appreciate the conception of this tower," quotes the Abbé Bulteau, "one will see that it is as frank as the execution is simple and skilful. Starting from the bottom, one reaches the summit of the flèche without marked break; without anything to interrupt the general form of the building. This clocher, whose base is broad (pleine), massive, and free from ornament, transforms itself, as it springs, into a sharp spire with eight faces, without its being possible to say where the massive construction ends and the light construction begins."

One cannot compare Chartres directly with any of its contemporary rivals, but one can at least compare the old spire with the new one which stands opposite and rises above it. Perhaps you will like the new best. Built at a time which is commonly agreed to have had the highest standard of taste, it does not encourage tourist or artist to insist on setting up standards of his own against it. Begun in 1507, it was finished in 1517. The dome of Saint Peter's at Rome, over which Bramante and Raphael and Michael Angelo toiled, was building at the same time; Leonardo da Vinci was working at Amboise; Jean Bullant, Pierre Lescot, and their patron, Francis I, were beginning their architectural careers. Four hundred years, or thereabouts, separated the old spire from the new one; and four hundred more separate the new one from us. If Viollet-le-Duc, who himself built Gothic spires, had cared to compare his flèches at Clermont-Ferrand with the new flèche at Chartres, he might perhaps have given us a rule where "adresse" ceases to have charm, and where detail becomes tiresome; but in the want of a schoolmaster to lay down a law of taste, you can admire the new flèche as much as you please. Of course, one sees that the lines of the new tower are not clean, like those of the old; the devices that cover the transition from the square to the octagon are rather too obvious; the proportion of the flèche to the tower quite alters the values of the parts; a rigid classical taste might even go so far as to hint that the new tower, in comparison with the old, showed signs of a certain tendency toward a dim and distant vulgarity. There can be no harm in admitting that the new tower is a little wanting in repose for a tower whose business is to counterpoise the very classic lines of the old one; but no law compels you to insist on absolute repose in any form of art; if such a law existed, it would have to deal with Michael Angelo before it dealt with us. The new tower has many faults, but it has great beauties, as you can prove by comparing it with other late Gothic spires, including those of Viollet-le-Duc. Its chief fault is to be where it is. As a companion to the crusades and to Saint Bernard, it lacks austerity. As a companion to the Virgin of Chartres, it recalls Diane de Poitiers.

In fact, the new tower, which in years is four centuries younger than its neighbour, is in feeling fully four hundred years older. It is self-conscious if not vain; its coiffure is elaborately arranged to cover the effects of age, and its neck and shoulders are covered with lace and jewels to hide a certain sharpness of skeleton. Yet it may be beautiful, still; the poets derided the wrinkles of Diane de Poitiers at the very moment when King Henry II idealized her with the homage of a Don Quixote; an atmosphere of physical beauty and decay hangs about the whole Renaissance.

One cannot push these resemblances too far, even for the twelfth century and the old tower. Exactly what date the old tower represents, as a social symbol, is a question that might be as much disputed as the beauty of Diane de Poitiers, and yet half the interest of architecture consists in the sincerity of its reflection of the society that builds. In mere time, by actual date, the old tower represents the second crusade, and when, in 1150, Saint Bernard was elected chief of that crusade in this very cathedral—or rather, in the cathedral of 1120, which was burned—the workmen were probably setting in mortar the stones of the flèche as we now see them; yet the flèche does not represent Saint Bernard in feeling, for Saint Bernard held the whole array of church-towers in horror as signs merely of display, wealth and pride. The flèche rather represents Abbot Suger of Saint-Denis, Abbot Peter the Venerable of Cluny, Abbot Abélard of Saint-Gildas-de-Rhuys, and Queen Eleanor of Guienne, who had married Louis-le-Jeune in 1137; who had taken the cross from Saint Bernard in 1147; who returned from the Holy Land in 1149; and who compelled Saint Bernard to approve her divorce in 1152. Eleanor and Saint Bernard were centuries apart, yet they lived at the same time and in the same church. Speaking exactly, the old tower represents neither of them; the new tower itself is hardly more florid than Eleanor was; perhaps less so, if one can judge from the fashions of the court-dress of her time. The old tower is almost Norman, while Eleanor was wholly Gascon, and Gascony was always florid without being always correct. The new tower, if it had been built in 1150, like the old one, would have expressed Eleanor perfectly, even in height and apparent effort to dwarf its mate, except that Eleanor dwarfed her husband without effort, and both in art and in history the result lacked in harmony.

Be the contrast what it may, it does not affect the fact that no other church in France has two spires that need be discussed in comparison with these. Indeed, no other cathedral of the same class has any spires at all, and this superiority of Chartres gave most of its point to a saying that "with the spires of Chartres, the choir of Beauvais, the nave of Amiens, and the façade of Rheims," one could make a perfect church—for us tourists.

It is true, after all, that one thing a historian clearly does, and that Henry Adams does too, is assign dates to things. He gives us plain "facts," and in this respect he writes at times like a particularly thorough tourist handbook or an encyclopedia. Thus Adams' third paragraph is devoted simply to dating the old tower (1091–1170) and the old part of the façade generally ("about 1150"). Here is information for us to note down and commit to memory if we like. But the question we have been asking is: What else does a good historian do? Does he *see* his world simply as a series of identifications in a chronological number system, or are the relations he is interested in more complicated than that?

It would be a mistake, of course, to generalize about all good historians from this passage by Adams, but at least we can say what Adams does with his terms besides mere dating. Before we try to define what that is, we had better make sure we know at least some of Adams' names and dates. Here is a scheme with some information we need to have.

Cathedral of Notre-Dame at Chartres

NEW OR NORTH TOWER (*on left in photograph*)	OLD OR SOUTH TOWER (*on right in photograph*)
constructed 1507–1517 Henry II, born 1519; King of France, 1547–59	constructed 1091–1170 Saint Bernard, 1090?–1153; preached Second Crusade
Diane de Poitiers, 1499–1566, mistress of Henry II with strong political influence over him	Eleanor of Aquitaine, 1122–1204, queen of Louis VII of France, later of Henry II of England, strong-minded, politically able, patroness of courtly literature and art

Now what does Adams make of these names and dates that might go beyond the simple assigning of numbers to people or objects? First, and very important, he *looks* with great care at the two towers, and uses his looking to make further relations. We can see what sort of relations these are by studying his elaborate contrast between the two towers in the last four paragraphs of the passage. He begins by giving each tower a character, a personality, a "feeling" that is derived from his own contemplation of details of the two structures. This feeling is outside of time—it is any time. "One sees that the lines of the new tower are not clean, like those of the old; the devices that cover the transition from the square to the octagon are rather too obvious." (Can *you* see these things, on the photograph?) There is even, he hints, "a certain tendency toward a dim and distant vulgarity." Here we can see the early stages of a metaphor that Adams is going to develop at some length— namely, the new tower seen as a person, specifically as a woman, a sort of royal whore. The tower has "great beauties," but "its chief fault is to be where it is. As a companion to the crusades and to Saint Bernard, it lacks austerity." The crusades and the saintly Bernard, of course, were contemporaries of the *old* tower, of which the new one is such an uncomfortable "companion." "As a companion to the Virgin of Chartres, it recalls Diane de Poitiers."

We all know who the Virgin was, and we can begin to see why Adams considers the new tower rather too vulgar for her. But who was Diane de Poitiers? If you knew nothing about her but her dates (contemporary with the new tower), you could perhaps learn almost all you needed to know from the next paragraph. The new tower, though younger "in years," is older "in feeling," and Diane de Poitiers, vain and powerful mistress of Henry II, becomes for Adams a *term* with which to *see* the feeling of the tower. The metaphor proceeds: "It is self-conscious if not vain; its coiffure is elaborately arranged to cover the effects of age, and its neck and shoulders are covered with lace and jewels to hide a certain sharpness of skeleton." You might try to see some of these things for yourself in the photograph: coiffure, lace and jewels, sharpness of skeleton. You might also note in our list of dates that Diane de Poitiers was born twenty years before her royal lover; she must have been able to "cover the effects of age" with considerable skill.

So much then for the new tower, which is defined not only chronologically but also "in feeling," by becoming associated metaphorically with a famous woman of the time who offers a useful way of seeing this piece of architecture. The old tower proves to be more difficult. "Yet half the interest of architecture consists in the sincerity of its reflection of the society that builds," so we try as we can to *characterize* this tower in the same way, by associating it with a contemporary figure. It doesn't work. Saint Bernard won't do; he was too pure even for this purest of churches. Queen Eleanor of Guienne (or Aquitaine) is suggested, the most powerful and energetic woman of the time. But she won't do either, being far too "florid" a figure for the simplicity of the old tower. "Speaking exactly, the old tower represents neither of them." It defies this sort of analysis, perhaps, in the way that the whole façade seemed to defy James.

At this point we might pause to ask what it means, in Adams' sense here, to "speak exactly." To speak exactly is to speak of *more* than dates. Obviously, if mere dating were the whole issue, then a label like "mid-twelfth-century" would satisfactorily "cover" Saint Bernard, Eleanor, and the old tower, all three. But for Adams such a label is by itself nowhere near satisfactory. A lot of other distinctions are at stake: aesthetic ones about architecture, and moral ones about people in history. "Eleanor and Saint Bernard were centuries apart, yet they lived at the same time and in the same church." The double use Adams makes of time is nowhere more evident than in this sentence. They lived at the same time *in years,* but they were centuries apart *in feeling.* And now Adams turns things around to some extent, by using a vocabulary of time to describe someone who did *not* live in that time. Eleanor, he says (to "speak exactly"), was like the *new* tower, like the mid-sixteenth century, four hundred years after her actual life span. So finally, in this brand of history, a whole period is given a kind of personality, a feeling. While he makes these vast relations, however, the tone of the author's voice, which has many touches of easy informality, reminds us not to take these equations as God-given truths, but as one man's way of coming to *terms* with the past.

Adams concludes the passage with a reference to "us tourists," an example of this easy tone. From what we have just observed, you may conclude that this is another mask, a self-consciously modest pose, like Mark Twain's posture of ignorance in chapter 4. Adams too is certainly no ordinary tourist; in fact he is hardly a tourist at all. Instead, he is using language as a particularly imaginative and sensitive historical writer, and that is the leap you are asked to take in composing essay 10.

Directions for Essay 10

Go back to the church whose façade you described in essay 9; and resee that façade in language a historian might use. You may undertake all the research you want, as to dates and so on, but your success will depend not on the accuracy of a set of guidebook facts, but on your ability to recreate this façade through appropriate use of historical metaphor.

The practical requirements which underlie every historical judgment give to all history the character of "contemporary history" because, however remote in time events there recounted may seem to be, the history in reality refers to present needs and present situations wherein those events vibrate.

CROCE

Chapter
11
History
as Ways
of Looking

The article that follows was written by a young man who at the time of writing was a teacher of history at Columbia. He considers here some of the difficulties that confront the historian, and he begins with a question—"What is a historical fact?" As usual, your problem is to relate the words of this article to your own experience as an amateur writer of history yourself. As you study the article, therefore, keep before you your own essay 10, and try to find in your own writing some examples of problems the article discusses. A few of its key terms are: historical fact, frame of reference or theory of history, cause, relativity of history. Your task in essay 11, then, will be to scrutinize your own language in relation to some of these words and phrases.

The Relativity of History

CHARLES WOOLSEY COLE

The question arises, "What is a historical fact?" The answer is that it is, at its best, what the historian thinks of what some one else thinks he saw or said or did or heard. At its worst it is a paltry third- or fourth-hand judgment. Psychology will have to develop much further before it can be known what relation something which has passed through the central neural processes of at least two men has to any objective reality. Still, such "facts" are at their simplest fairly clear-cut. The more they deal with complex situations, with motives, causes, effects, changes or connections, the more nebulous they become. But that is not all, for the very simplest and clearest historical fact, when isolated, has little meaning. It has to be tied to other facts to bring out its importance. When, however, it comes to a question of selecting, relating and ordering facts, history becomes essentially subjective. In short, the relation between any page of history and some objective reality which once existed is tenuous. The meaning and significance of that page are in large part, at least, the results of subjective processes of the historian's mind. With all the will to objectivity in the world, with all the honesty that can be conceived, with all the desire to tell things exactly as they happened, the historian cannot produce work which has at the same time significance and a close relationship to something that objectively existed in the past. . . .

The historical fact, *in itself,* has little significance. . . . If a frame of reference can be discovered and the historical fact related to it, perhaps the fact will be clothed in a new

From "The Relativity of History" in *Political Science Quarterly* 48, no. 2 (June 1933). Reprinted by permission of the *Quarterly* and the author.

meaning. That is just what historians have always tended to do, for it is a commonplace that every age writes its own history according to its own beliefs and ideas. From the beginning of the Christian era well into the seventeenth century, from Orosius to Cotton Mather, historians took their material and related it to their theories of a divine order, of the workings of God upon man, of man's search for eternal salvation. So related, facts were significant, and if an earthquake became a judgment of God, still the history as a whole had a meaning. In the eighteenth century historians related their facts to theories as to the rational order of nature, natural laws, the rights of man or the like. In the nineteenth century they gave their facts meaning by tying them to nationalist, democratic, socialist or evolutionary theories.

Today either historians give their facts significance by using explicitly one of the older theories, as Spengler has used and strained the biologic analogy; or other and perhaps newer theories are implicit in their work. They seek for objectivity, but they must select and order and interpret the facts. This they can do fairly and justly but they cannot do it without some theories in the light of which they may select and order and interpret. What is the social order and economic history of the present but history written under the influence of theories as to the paramount importance of the evolution of social and economic institutions and folkways? If the modern social historian could present his arguments to the Venerable Bede, that worthy might well shrug his shoulders and reply, "To me these things that you call social and economic are all very well, but I wish to see how it was that God ordained the conversion of the British Isles."

Historical facts, then, gain their meaning when by order, selection and interpretation they are related to a frame of reference. This frame of reference is a theory of, or a way of looking at history, explicit or implicit, old or new. Without relation to some theory the fact is an isolated entity of dubious validity and little meaning. Without some theory the historian cannot, from the immense mass of historical facts, select and order his material, or interpret what he has chosen and arranged. . . .

The remark is often heard, "We shall have to wait for the judgment of history on that," or "We are so close to this that we cannot write the history of it; we shall have to wait until time has given us the proper perspective." Such statements do not mean that contemporaries who share in events and know at least something of their psychological bases would not be the best ones to write the history of the era. Nor does it mean that the historian must wait hungrily until some government sees fit to disgorge a few incriminating documents, or until some statesman takes his pen in hand to write an unreliable apologia. They mean that the contemporary can see sequence but not causes. To write of causes the historian must wait until the material has shaken down into patterns, patterns not inherent in the events but arising gradually from the minds of men who in after years think about the events. While the historian waits for the formation of these patterns, the *Zeitgeist* dissolves, most of the material is lost and buried. But the historian must wait, for until the patterns, or theories of causation, are built up out of the scattered fragments of an era, he cannot write intelligible history which shows events proceeding from cause to effect. Events are linked in time and space, but the causal connections between them are evolved from the subjective processes of men who think about them.

The very idea of causation is injected from without into an incoherent mass of chance-ordained events by the historian's processes of selection, ordering and interpretation. Causes in written history proceed not from any objective reality on which the writing is based, but from a subjective adherence by the historian to some theory or frame of reference to which he can relate his facts. Yet the historian should not flinch before the idea that the material with which he deals is in actuality chance-ordained, when it is becoming more apparent all the time that the basic processes of nature must be described in terms of chance and not of mechanical determinism. . . .

If, then, the significance of historical facts—and the same reasoning might be applied to the data of the other social sciences—together with their causal connections and their continuity proceed from their being related to some frame of reference, which is to say some implicit or explicit theory, the position of a theory in history becomes quite different. In the past theories have been tested by the supposedly empirical method of referring them to the "facts of history," that is, by referring them to rather misty entities which take on meaning, continuity, or connection only in the light of the theories themselves. If it should happen that the new point of view based on hints from the recent work in the physical sciences should come to be adopted, the theories of history would be placed consciously in a respectable and stable position. No longer would they cringe and cower like handmaidens before the queenly "facts." For they would be tested not only by the facts, but by pragmatic criteria as to whether they served their purpose of giving in abundance to the facts of history significance, connection and continuity, as to whether they became the foci of broad syntheses which tended from a practical and from a pedagogic point of view to make history intelligible and valuable, and finally as to whether they conformed to similar theories in other fields of knowledge.

Practically, the adoption of such an attitude toward their material would mean that thinkers in history would in part turn their attention from delving after facts to an effort to build up theories and philosophies. As the work progressed theories would come and go and change, but gradually there might arise magnificent beacons in whose light human history would glow with renewed beauty, enhanced significance, close-knit interconnection and intelligible casuality.

When, in essay 10, you saw your church façade as a historian might see it, you could have interpreted your "historical facts" in any of a wide variety of ways. Yet if Mr. Cole's argument is a fair one, you could not have interpreted your facts without making use, perhaps unconsciously, of a "frame of reference" or "theory" of history. What is such a frame of reference? It is, Cole states, "a way of looking at history, explicit or implicit, old or new," and historians simply cannot operate "without some theories *in the light of which* they may select and order and interpret." (You observe that this article, like many other passages in this book, makes repeated use of "looking" and "light" as metaphors for intellectual activity; the beacons in the final sentence are a shining example.) Now the question is, what particular "light" did you make use of in essay 10, in order to "look" at your church façade in historical terms? For example, let us suppose that your church was of the puritan-New England sort, all clapboards and white pillars. You might have seen its façade, then, as simple and chaste, a maidenly expression of an uncomplicated faith with no sophisticated refinements or adornments. In that case you would be making a causal relation between a spiritual attitude (puritan simplicity and rigor) and an architectural form (clapboards and white pillars). And the light, the frame of reference or theory you would be drawing on would be one of *religious* history. But how easily you might have chosen some other light to illuminate some other relation. You could have turned yourself into an *economic* historian, for example, with quite a different theory of causation. The church in this case would be seen, not as a chaste and pious maiden, but as a practical barnlike structure of some crudity, and you would account for this by pointing not to religious beliefs, but to such "facts" as the lack of good masons in early New England, the abundance of forests for building materials, and the financial necessity of making do with an unadorned and inexpensive building. Why, finally, you choose the religious theory or the economic theory or some other as your favorite "light," the one you would be most disposed to see by and defend, is a question that can probably be answered only by the strictest introspection into your own values and thought processes.

Directions for Essay 11

Select a statement from your essay 10 in which you expressed or implied a causal relation between historical "facts." Show just what relation you were making: what fact caused what other fact? Then show what frame of reference or theory of history is suggested by the particular relation you made. What other theory of history might have prompted some other causal relation between the same two facts? Illustrate this other possibility in detail, and then show, if you can, why you chose originally the particular frame of reference you did rather than some other.

Chapter
12
Seeing
the Wind

In chapter 12 you are asked to "see" something that strictly speaking cannot be seen at all—the wind. The sensation of observing the wind is an everyday occurrence in your life. Can you say what it is like?

Here are three exceedingly different witnesses to various sorts of wind. The first is the famed "Ode to the West Wind" by Shelley. The poet, you'll observe, can address the wind directly —"thou breath of Autumn's being." The second is a portion of a lyric by Emily Dickinson. And the third is a journal account of a peculiar sort of local wind, the "Santa Ana" in Los Angeles.

We probably shouldn't claim that reading these passages will necessarily help you write a better essay. So read these or not, as you please. In any case, you'll be asked in the essay to put into words, as precisely as you can, some windy experience of your own.

Ode to the West Wind

PERCY BYSSHE SHELLEY

I

O wild West Wind, thou breath of Autumn's being,
Thou, from whose unseen presence the leaves dead
Are driven, like ghosts from an enchanter fleeing,

Yellow, and black, and pale, and hectic red,
Pestilence-stricken multitudes: O thou
Who chariotest to their dark wintry bed

The wingéd seeds, where they lie cold and low,
Each like a corpse within its grave, until
Thine azure sister of the Spring shall blow

Her clarion o'er the dreaming earth, and fill
(Driving sweet buds like flocks to feed in air)
With living hues and odours plain and hill:

Wild Spirit, which art moving everywhere;
Destroyer and Preserver; hear, oh, hear!

II

Thou on whose stream, mid·the steep sky's commotion,
Loose clouds like earth's decaying leaves are shed,
Shook from the tangled boughs of Heaven and Ocean,

Angels of rain and lightning: there are spread
On the blue surface of thine airy surge,
Like the bright hair uplifted from the head

Of some fierce Maenad, even from the dim verge
Of the horizon to the zenith's height,
The locks of the approaching storm. Thou dirge

Of the dying year, to which this closing night
Will be the dome of a vast sepulchre,
Vaulted with all thy congregated might

Of vapours, from whose solid atmosphere
Black rain, and fire, and hail, will burst: oh, hear!

III

Thou who didst waken from his summer dreams
The blue Mediterranean, where he lay,
Lulled by the coil of his crystalline streams,

Beside a pumice isle in Baiae's bay,
And saw in sleep old palaces and towers
Quivering within the wave's intenser day,

All overgrown with azure moss and flowers
So sweet, the sense faints picturing them! Thou
For whose path the Atlantic's level powers

Cleave themselves into chasms, while far below
The sea-blooms and the oozy woods which wear
The sapless foliage of the ocean, know

Thy voice, and suddenly grow gray with fear,
And tremble and despoil themselves: oh, hear!

IV

If I were a dead leaf thou mightest bear;
If I were a swift cloud to fly with thee;
A wave to pant beneath thy power, and share

The impulse of thy strength, only less free
Than thou, O uncontrollable! If even
I were as in my boyhood, and could be

The comrade of thy wanderings over Heaven,
As then, when to outstrip the skyey speed
Scarce seemed a vision; I would ne'er have striven

As thus with thee in prayer in my sore need.
Oh, lift me as a wave, a leaf, a cloud!
I fall upon the thorns of life! I bleed!

A heavy weight of hours has chained and bowed
One too like thee: tameless, and swift, and proud.

v

Make me thy lyre even as the forest is:
What if my leaves are falling like its own!
The tumult of thy mighty harmonies

Will take from both a deep, autumnal tone,
Sweet though in sadness. Be thou, Spirit fierce,
My spirit! Be thou me, impetuous one!

Drive my dead thought over the universe
Like withered leaves to quicken a new birth!
And, by the incantation of this verse,

Scatter, as from an unextinguished hearth
Ashes and sparks, my words among mankind!
Be through my lips to unawakened earth

The trumpet of a prophecy! O Wind,
If Winter comes, can Spring be far behind?

FROM **#109**

EMILY DICKINSON

Of all the sounds despatched abroad,
There's not a Charge to me
Like that old measure in the Boughs—
That phraseless Melody—

The Wind does—working like a Hand,
Whose fingers Comb the Sky—
Then quiver down—with tufts of Tune—
Permitted Gods, and me—

Los Angeles Notebook

JOAN DIDION

There is something uneasy in the Los Angeles air
this afternoon, some unnatural stillness, some tension. What it
means is that tonight a Santa Ana will begin to blow, a hot
wind from the northeast whining down through the Cajon and
San Gorgonio Passes, blowing up sandstorms out along Route
66, drying the hills and the nerves to the flash point. For a few
days now we will see smoke back in the canyons, and hear
sirens in the night. I have neither heard nor read that a Santa
Ana is due, but I know it, and almost everyone I have seen
today knows it too. We know it because we feel it. The baby
frets. The maid sulks. I rekindle a waning argument with the
telephone company, then cut my losses and lie down, given
over to whatever it is in the air. To live with the Santa Ana is
to accept, consciously or unconsciously, a deeply mechanistic
view of human behavior.

I recall being told, when I first moved to Los Angeles and
was living on an isolated beach, that the Indians would throw
themselves into the sea when the bad wind blew. I could see
why. The Pacific turned ominously glossy during a Santa Ana
period, and one woke in the night troubled not only by the
peacocks screaming in the olive trees but by the eerie absence
of surf. The heat was surreal. The sky had a yellow cast, the

kind of light sometimes called "earthquake weather." My only neighbor would not come out of her house for days, and there were no lights at night, and her husband roamed the place with a machete. One day he would tell me that he had heard a trespasser, the next a rattlesnake.

"On nights like that," Raymond Chandler once wrote about the Santa Ana, "every booze party ends in a fight. Meek little wives feel the edge of the carving knife and study their husbands' necks. Anything can happen." That was the kind of wind it was. I did not know then that there was any basis for the effect it had on all of us, but it turns out to be another of those cases in which science bears out folk wisdom. The Santa Ana, which is named for one of the canyons it rushes through, is a *foehn* wind, like the *foehn* of Austria and Switzerland and the *hamsin* of Israel. There are a number of persistent malevolent winds, perhaps the best known of which are the mistral of France and the Mediterranean sirocco, but a *foehn* wind has distinct characteristics: it occurs on the leeward slope of a mountain range and, although the air begins as a cold mass, it is warmed as it comes down the mountain and appears finally as a hot dry wind. Whenever and wherever a *foehn* blows, doctors hear about headaches and nausea and allergies, about "nervousness," about "depression." In Los Angeles some teachers do not attempt to conduct formal classes during a Santa Ana, because the children become unmanageable. In Switzerland the suicide rate goes up during the *foehn*, and in the courts of some Swiss cantons the wind is considered a mitigating circumstance for crime. Surgeons are said to watch the wind, because blood does not clot normally during a *foehn*. A few years ago an Israeli physicist discovered that not only during such winds, but for the ten or twelve hours which precede them, the air carries an unusually high ratio of positive to negative ions. No one seems to know exactly why that should be; some talk about friction and others suggest solar disturbances. In any case the positive ions are there, and what an excess of positive ions does, in the simplest terms, is make people unhappy. One cannot get much more mechanistic than that.

Easterners commonly complain that there is no "weather" at all in Southern California, that the days and the seasons slip by relentlessly, numbingly bland. That is quite misleading. In fact the climate is characterized by infrequent but violent extremes: two periods of torrential subtropical rains which continue for weeks and wash out the hills and send subdivisions sliding toward the sea; about twenty scattered days a year of the Santa Ana, which, with its incendiary dryness, invariably means fire. At the first prediction of a Santa Ana, the Forest Service flies men and equipment from northern California into the southern forests, and the Los Angeles Fire Department cancels its ordinary non-firefighting routines. The Santa Ana caused Malibu to burn the way it did in 1956, and Bel Air in 1961, and Santa Barbara in 1964. In the winter of 1966–67 eleven men were killed fighting a Santa Ana fire that spread through the San Gabriel Mountains.

Just to watch the front-page news out of Los Angeles during a Santa Ana is to get very close to what it is about the place. The longest single Santa Ana period in recent years was in 1957, and it lasted not the usual three or four days but fourteen days, from November 21 until December 4. On the first day 25,000 acres of the San Gabriel Mountains were burning, with gusts reaching 100 miles an hour. In town, the wind reached Force 12, or hurricane force, on the Beaufort Scale; oil derricks were toppled and people ordered off the downtown streets to avoid injury from flying objects. On November 22 the fire in the San Gabriels was out of control. On November 24 six people were killed in automobile accidents, and by the end of the week the Los Angeles *Times* was keeping a box score of traffic deaths. On November 26 a prominent Pasadena attorney, depressed about money, shot and killed his wife, their two sons, and himself. On November 27 a South Gate divorcée, twenty-two, was murdered and thrown from a moving car. On November 30 the San Gabriel fire was still out of control, and the wind in town was blowing eighty miles an hour. On the first day of December four people died violently, and on the third the wind began to break.

It is hard for people who have not lived in Los Angeles to realize how radically the Santa Ana figures in the local imagination. The city burning is Los Angeles's deepest image of itself: Nathanael West perceived that, in *The Day of the Locust*; and at the time of the 1965 Watts riots what struck the imagination most indelibly were the fires. For days one could drive the Harbor Freeway and see the city on fire, just as we had always known it would be in the end. Los Angeles weather is the weather of catastrophe, of apocalypse, and, just as the realiably long and bitter winters of New England determine the way life is lived there, so the violence and the unpredictability of the Santa Ana affect the entire quality of life in Los Angeles, accentuate its impermanence, its unreliability. The wind shows us how close to the edge we are.

Directions for Essay 12

Take a stand at a particular place and time, and describe the wind just as thoroughly as you can. Try it in verse if you like.

> *The world is in a constant flux around and in us, but in order to grapple with the floating reality we create in our thought, or at any rate in our language, certain more or less fixed points, certain averages. Reality never presents us with an average but language does.*
>
> OTTO JESPERSEN

Chapter
13
Wind
as Science

Of course there are a thousand ways to see the wind. You can even talk to it—"O wild West Wind," cries Shelley. The terms available for describing the wind are practically infinite, and one reason for this may be, as we have already pointed out, that you can't see wind at all, directly. All you can do is sense it through signs: rustling of leaves, blowing of smoke, cool sensation on your face. You interpret certain feelings that your senses give you, and you call that wind. To recall the language of chapter 4, you observe the world around you and *read* it as wind.

In this next exercise you are going to try to see wind in one particular set of terms—the terms of numbers. To see things as numbers, to "measure" things, is a way of seeing that enjoys enormous prestige in our time, and it suggests all the dramatic improvements of life that have accompanied the growth of science. Whatever else it is that scientists do, one thing they obviously do is measure things, so that the world becomes defined in relation to an organization of statistical language.

How can you express the wind statistically? You have to have a device, an instrument of some sort, and in the case of measuring the speed of the wind, this instrument is called an anemometer. Then you communicate your various readings of this instrument by making use of a scale of measurement. Here, for example, is a famous scale of measurement—one invented by an Admiral Beaufort in 1806. (It is mentioned in Joan Didion's "Los Angeles Notebook," chapter 12.) As you study it, try to determine what instrument Beaufort has selected for his readings. What was Beaufort's anemometer?

Beaufort Number	Description of the Wind	Beaufort's Criteria	
0	Calm		
1	Light Air	Just sufficient to give steerage way	
2	Light Breeze	with which a well-conditioned	1 to 2 knots
3	Gentle Breeze	man-of-war under all sail, and	3 to 4 knots
4	Moderate Breeze	clean full, would go in smooth	5 to 6 knots
		water from	
5	Fresh Breeze		Royals, etc.
6	Strong Breeze	in which the same	Single-reefs & topgallants
7	Moderate Gale	ship could just	Double-reefs, jibs, etc.
8	Fresh Gale	carry close hauled	Triple-reefs, courses, etc.
9	Strong Gale		Close-reefs and courses
10	Whole Gale	with which she could only bear close-reefed main topsail and reefed foresail.	
11	Storm	with which she could be reduced to storm staysails.	
12	Hurricane	to which she could show no canvas.	

Beaufort's anemometer was of course "a well-conditioned man-of-war," with all her complications of sails and rigging. That is the instrument he reads with this scale. For example, if the wind were blowing so hard that such a ship could just carry close-hauled single reefs and topgallants, then we are to name that wind a "Strong Breeze" or Beaufort 6. And what is the advantage of such naming? One advantage you can readily appreciate simply by casting your eye down the left-hand row of numbers and comparing their brevity with the vastly more cumbersome phrasing under the headings "Description of the Wind" and "Beaufort's Criteria." The numbers are so simple! They are so easy to tell to someone else, so easy for a ship captain to enter in his log. Yet they are also, perhaps you will want to object, *too* simple. "Beaufort 6" is not an adequate translation of "Strong breeze in which a well-conditioned man-of-war could just carry close-hauled single-reefs and topgallants." To this objection one can only say that this always happens when life is expressed in statistics, or indeed any simple terms. There is a great gain in ease of communication; there is a great loss in richness and precision. Notice the paradox that numbers are actually *im*precise, inasmuch as they fail to show the indefiniteness of actual experience. This is a constant problem in science, and it occurs in all acts of measurement, even when the instrument being read and recorded with pencil and paper is, say, a needle on a dial, and not a well-conditioned man-of-war. The physicist, P. W. Bridgman, has put it this way: "Any physical indefiniteness does not get into the paper and pencil operations because the first preliminary to the paper and pencil operations is to replace the instrumental indications by numbers mathematically sharp." The sharpness, then, the clarity and simplicity, are in the mathematics, not in the wind. It would be hard to overemphasize this truth.

Now how can you proceed as a scientist, however amateur, and see wind numerically? You will need an anemometer, and you will not find it convenient to use a well-conditioned man-of-war. You will have to make your own instrument, and invent a scale of measurement to use with it. Your terms will not be "Beaufort 1–2–3," or miles per hour, but your own: "Smith 1–2–3," "O'Callahan 1–2–3." Before going ahead with this project it will be helpful for you to read a few pages from a standard meteorological text of some years ago in which wind and various methods and difficulties of measuring it are discussed.

Wind

SIR NAPIER SHAW

The chief element in the structure of the atmosphere is the wind, the motion of the air. It is also the most difficult to visualise from fixed instruments, designed for the express purpose, under the general name of anemometers, because all such instruments have to be attached to some structure. Within the limit of height of all solid structures the motion of the air is complicated by the eddies due to what is called the friction of the ground, partly the actual resistance of fixed obstacles, hills, buildings, trees, etc., or moving obstacles, waves of water, etc., and partly to the molecular viscosity of the air which would still produce some effect even if the surface of the land or sea were perfectly level. . . . The layer of the atmosphere near the surface, where instruments for measuring the direction and velocity of the wind are of necessity installed, is most unsatisfactory for the purpose, and this opinion is amply justified by the extraordinary complication which the records of any anemometer disclose. Some are more complicated than others but all show some degree of complication, and the problem of obtaining an idea of the changes of the general atmospheric structure from the records of an anemometer is a very awkward one.

The number of anemometers designed for measuring or recording the direction and velocity of the wind is very large. . . . Meteorological practice has in the course of time concentrated its attention on two forms of anemometer, the

Robinson anemometer which consists of horizontal cross-arms with hemispherical cups at their ends, the rate of rotation of which is very nearly proportional to the "mean" velocity of the wind, and the Dines anemograph which, like the Pitot tube, depends upon the pressure exerted by the wind upon the opening of a tube. It is measured by some form of pressure-gauge always with the proviso that since a pressure-gauge has two openings, one for each side of the gauge, the instruments must make due allowance for the effect of the wind upon the second limb of the gauge. . . .

[Another] method of recording the force and direction of the wind is by means of a plate which is turned by a vane to face the wind and which records the force by the compression of a spring. This plan is used in Osler's anemometer which has been in continuous operation at the Royal Observatory, Greenwich since January 13, 1841. The records are published in the reports of the Observatory.

They ought to show a relation with the records of the Robinson anemograph not differing much from:

$$F = .003V^2,$$

where F is the pressure in lbs. per sq. ft. and V the velocity in miles per hour. They do not do so. The differences may perhaps be accounted for by the fact that the plate would adjust its record to the extremes of a transient gust and the anemograph shows only the smooth value. But that is only a partial explanation, the differences are too great. One of the curiosities of meteorological work upon wind is that differences of the kind here referred to are tolerated for years without anyone feeling it necessary to explore the subject to the point of actual conviction.

The secret of that really intolerable toleration is the basic difficulty of all anemographic records—the exposure. The reading of any anemograph is a function not only of the instrument but of the site, and of the shape and orientation of the structure upon which the instrument is mounted. Any flat vertical surface exposed to the wind produces a localised eddy analogous to what is treated elsewhere as a cliff-eddy, and a few degrees of difference in the orientation of the wind may have a considerable effect on the record. The conclusion arrived at in the Meteorological Office was that nothing short of a separate structure, a tower of open ironwork, on a very open space of level ground was really efficient and even in that case . . . distant geographical features may have a paramount influence upon the record of the wind. . . .

Hence it has come about that unless the local opportunity for exposure was exceptionally good it was not thought desirable to insist upon, or even to advise, the erection of an elaborate instrument for recording the wind. Wind did not really lend itself to recording, except in a specially local sense, local as to building as well as site and general locality. It was thought better to get the general impression of the wind which is expressed by the adaptation of the Beaufort scale to observations on land than to obtain a more precise numerical value which had no meteorological significance of the same order of accuracy. No structure of meteorological reasoning can be raised without a tolerance of at least 20 percent in the assigned values of surface-winds.

The reader may be surprised to learn that measuring the wind is really a most difficult operation, but he may realise the truth of the statement when he understands that thirty years ago, on account of the inherent difficulty of the subject, the Meteorological Office has to be content to publish values of wind-velocity which were known to be in error by 25 percent, and even now the quotation, without reference, of a reading of an anemometer from a considerable number of meteorological publications is no guarantee that an error of that order of magnitude is not involved.

.   .   .

Gustiness and Eddies

When the tube-anemometer, devised by W. H. Dines in 1890, was set in operation the wind was seen from the records to consist of a series of rapid alternations of velocity, and when a direction-recorder was subsequently added the alternations in velocity were found to be accompanied by corresponding alternations in direction.

We have stated the general problem of the meteorological calculus as being the interpretation of the record of a pressure-tube anemometer with the understanding that the incidents of history recorded in the trace, in so far as they can be regarded as referring to entities with a certain validity, are probably the result of some analogy in the local motion of the air to the rotation of a solid. We may recognise something which bears out this suggestion in shiftiness, in gustiness, in squalls, whirlwinds and tornadoes, and the suggestions of revolving fluid to be found in the isobars of weathermaps.

Our first business is with the gustiness and shiftiness which is the common characteristic of anemometer records when there is a reasonable flow.

It is agreed that the gustiness so recorded is due to turbulence: that turbulence is eddy-motion treated statistically, quite unrestricted as to the three dimensions, horizontal and vertical; and that an eddy represents the effort of spin to preserve the identity of the parcel of air which has been made to spin with some analogy to a revolving solid by the interference of an obstacle of some sort with the steady flow of current.

Anemograph records make it quite clear that the effect of the eddies which are expressed statistically as turbulence is of the same order of magnitude as the flow, sometimes annihilating it or even reversing it and sometimes doubling its speed. . . .

A permanent eddy is formed at the edges of cliffs or the ridges of houses or walls in all strong winds. The reader can make experiments for himself, simply with an empty match box or even his own hat, in the eddy formed by a strong wind blowing upon a nearly vertical cliff. A most remarkable example of a cliff-eddy can be found at the Rock of Gibraltar when a strong levanter blows on the steep eastern face of the Rock. Its effect upon the tube-anemometer which was maintained at the signal station on the Rock was very remarkable. When the velocity of the wind reached a certain limit it passed the opening of the anemometer in a direction nearly vertical and the effect was a reduction of the pressure in the recording float. A limit is thus fixed to the velocity which the instrument can record and gusts of greater velocity appear on the record as entirely fictitious lulls, due to the withdrawal of the pen to the zero line by the "suction" of the air passing the anemometer.

As Sir Napier says, "measuring the wind is really a most difficult operation." Now try it.

Directions for Essay 13

Build your own anemometer. Use paper clips, cardboard, pencil stubs, Ping-Pong balls, whatever your ingenuity can devise. Write a careful account of how you built your anemometer. Then run a series of tests with it, using a scale of measurement of your own invention. Describe these tests. What would you say was scientific about this experience? What was not scientific?

Go, wondrous creature! mount where Science guides,
Go, measure earth, weigh air, and state the tides.

POPE

Chapter
14
The Human
Standpoint

The author of the following article on the "revolution" in modern physics a generation ago is not a professional scientist—he is a professor of English. In the book from which this passage is taken, called *Science and Criticism*, Mr. Muller presents himself as a "layman" or even as a "literary fellow." He is consciously concerned, therefore, with making connections between science and other "lay" areas of activity, and that, of course, is one of the principal aims of a liberal arts student in becoming acquainted with scientific ways of doing things.

You have just completed a modest experience in a kind of scientific activity—measuring the wind. As you read this article, try to make its terms relevant to your recent experience. No one would want to say that your homemade anemometer and a physicist's latest atom-smasher are in most senses comparable instruments. Still, your situation as a measurer of wind was not so thoroughly remote from the situation of serious scientists as you may have supposed.

The Revolution in Physics

HERBERT J. MULLER

"See Mystery to Mathematics fly!" wrote Pope in a simpler age. Today the layman who attempts to follow the flight through the probability waves in the time-space continuum is apt to appreciate the blessed old mysteries. The chief trouble is that he really wants to *see*. He lives in a common-sense world full of material things and uses a language full of nouns, which by definition are "substantives" or names of these things. Stubbornly he asks, What *is* an electromagnetic field? what *is* a line of force? To such questions physicists are blandly indifferent. They still tolerate "matter" but only on sufferance; many look forward to a day in which they can dispense with this "theoretical construction" and explain everything in terms of "field"—although this too is not necessarily "real." In general, they do not care what their symbols "stand for" so long as they can get handier equations. Space has the physical property of transmitting electromagnetic waves, Einstein tells us, and we should not "bother too much about the meaning of this statement."

Yet one need not fly all the way to mathematics to catch the main idea of what is going on—the specific equations will probably have been revised before he has got to them anyway. The permanent contribution of modern physics lies in its new base of operations. Between the calculations of Newton and Einstein there is only a slight difference; for all ordinary purposes one can still measure things in the old-time way. Between the implications of their theories, however, there is an enormous difference. And this difference, in which lies the

From *Science and Criticism* by Herbert J. Muller, copyright 1943 by Yale University Press. Reprinted by permission of the publishers.

profoundest revolution of an age noisy with revolutions, the layman can grasp.

In its main outlines, the story of what has happened is familiar enough. Classical physics explained everything in terms of matter and motion in Euclidean space, running the ancient forms of Being by as immutable a clockwork mechanism. From the beginning there were troublesome fictions, such as the apparently jelly-like "ether" that transmitted light but somehow offered no resistance to the wheeling spheres; yet the whole scheme was built solidly on common sense, and it seemed to work beautifully. The first principles of physics were accordingly regarded as a priori, its framework and method as inevitable and inalterable. Jealous philosophers kept raising questions, asking how our senses enabled us to be so intimate with the little lumps of matter and how these lumps kept pushing one another around, but the very success of scientists resulted from their indifference to such questions, their naïve acceptance of a faith without bothering to explain or justify it. In time, however, they accumulated more and more experimental data—especially regarding electricity—that could not be explained satisfactorily by their mechanistic concepts. Clerk Maxwell's brilliant electromagnetic theory of light did *not* have a mechanical basis, yet it also seemed to work. Hence their very successes finally forced scientists to look to their faith. And even as Renan was exclaiming, "The world today has no more mysteries!" this tidy world was crumbling.

The story may conveniently begin with one of the greatest but least known of Russian revolutionists, the mathematician Lobachevsky. Euclid's axiom, that through a given point only one parallel could be drawn to a given line, had been considered a fact of nature, plain to the eye. But in 1826 Lobachevsky, as if just for the hell of it, denied this self-evident truth—and built up a whole consistent geometry on the assumption that *more* than one parallel could be drawn through this point. Then another mathematician constructed a new geometry on the assumption that *no* such parallel could be drawn; and thus there developed flocks of geometries. These have in turn proved useful to physicists. (In quantum theory, I gather, profitable use has been made of an arithmetic in which 2 times 3 does not equal 3 times 2.) Accordingly they too changed their base of operations. Einstein challenged the axiom of simultaneity, that two events can happen in *different* places at the *same* time, and thereby developed his theory of relativity. All along the line physicists have arrived at more satisfactory interpretations of experimental facts by scrapping self-evident truths, breaking the laws of thought—by a systematic exploitation, as it were, of the nonsense that the eighteenth century had triumphantly eliminated. They pride themselves chiefly on the possibility of asking still more preposterous questions and getting still more preposterous answers.

The important contribution of modern physics, then, is not the particular nonsense that it will erect into the truth of tomorrow. It is the junking of Newton's absolutes, the breaking up of his or any other fixed frame of reference, the overthrow of the totalitarian state in the world of thought and the establishment of a democracy in which all hypotheses are freely elected. The revolution might be summarized as the triumph of the postulate over the axiom. An axiom is something self-evident, fixed, unquestioned. A postulate is something assumed, to be tested for its usefulness—not a law laid down by God but a logical fiction consciously invented by man. "No one can say," declared Descartes of the properties of triangles, "that I have invented or imagined them"; mathematicians and scientists now say just this. We must be very careful, writes P. W. Bridgman, that "our present experience does not exact hostages of the future." This might seem too squeamish a concern for posterity, which can be trusted to take care of itself; but scientists are concerned chiefly with their own experience. Newton's assumption of Absolute Time had restricted their outlook and course of action for some two hundred years.

To come to the more specific concepts, it is common news that "matter" is no longer the inert, grossly "material" stuff of old. Physicists now represent objects as processes or events, trace dynamic patterns of an intricacy and subtlety that make the traditional operations of spirit seem crude. The most familiar element in our experience, matter has become more and more elusive, mysterious, incomprehensible. Further, the scientific definition of it is generally conceived as an idealization—a convenient formula, in Bertrand Russell's words, "for describing what happens where it isn't." Strictly, physicists do not know what they are talking about. They do not know what anything *is;* they tell us only what something *does.* Their descriptions are not photographs but ordnance maps for future operations. In a sense, accordingly, they do not so much uncover truth as create it. In *The Evolution of Physics* Einstein talks constantly of the "important invention" of the electromagnetic field and all the other realities "created by modern physics." He rejoices in the new concepts because they have enabled us "to create a more subtle reality"; he would therefore drop them instantly for concepts that made possible a still fancier reality. In other words, the reality known to man is not immutable.

It follows that scientific "laws" are not categorical imperatives. As Karl Pearson pointed out, they are shorthand descriptions of nature and cannot be said to *rule* it. That nature appears to obey them proves nothing, for they were invented for just that purpose; when more experimental returns come in, nature will obey some new, perhaps quite different laws. To give a new twist to the old religious argument, law indeed implies a Lawgiver—who is Man. At any moment, moreover, there are various conceivable ways of interpreting the experimental data. Physicists always prefer the widest possible generalization and the simplest possible formula, seek to break nature down into as few elements and laws as they can; but this procedure is a convenient method, not an absolute necessity. "Nature is pleased with simplicity,"

Newton wrote, and certainly men are pleased with it; but of nature we cannot be sure. The latest investigations of the subatomic world suggest to physicists as well as laymen that it may be complex beyond the dreams of Marcel Proust.

Implied in these statements is again the human "standpoint." Alfred Korzybski makes out, roughly, three periods in the history of thought: the Greek period, metaphysical and idealistic, in which emphasis was primarily on the observer; the scientific period, semiempirical and materialistic, in which emphasis was primarily on the thing observed; and the period now dawning, in which knowledge is a transaction between the observer and the observed. On the submicroscopic level, quantum physicists are confirming Coleridge's suspicion of the mechanistic assumption of inert matter that can be observed without being disturbed. The quantum of energy leaving the electron and hitting the observer's eye can be measured only by a new observation, which in turn affects the electron; we cannot actually peep into the private life of the electron. On the cosmic level, Einstein has assumed that absolute time is as meaningless as absolute length or absolute cheese, and that all possible measurements of time and space necessarily involve our position. As Bridgman says, he seized on "the act of the observer as the essence of the situation." The world of Planck and Einstein seems strange, indeed, precisely because man cannot be left out of it. He is not only the most intricate but an indispensable piece of apparatus.

To admit the importance of the observer is also, however, to admit that approximateness is a necessary condition of human knowledge, not merely a matter of imperfect instruments. Uncertainty or mere probability has therefore been erected into a scientific principle. In classical physics one could, in theory, predict with absolute accuracy the future course of any bit of matter if one knew its position and velocity and the forces acting upon it. Heisenberg's Principle of Indeterminacy states that because of the very nature of things we cannot possibly know *both* the position and the velocity of any bit, and that the more precisely we determine the one, the less we must know about the other. Furthermore, in quantum physics there are no laws for the behavior of an individual particle but only statistical averages, "bookkeeping laws," for the behavior of the whole crowd. The physicist cannot even in theory make a definite appointment with a particular electron; he can state merely the probability of where and when it will turn up. He knows that in a certain period approximately so many radium atoms will disintegrate, but he does not know which ones are doomed, or why, or precisely when they will meet their fate. Hence another striking paradox: in this view the lawfulness of nature may be rooted in lawlessness, a very high degree of uniformity resulting only because billions of coins are tossed. What the physicist can state with mathematical exactness is the limits of the *in*exactness of his calculations; as in all operations of pure chance on a large scale, there is a predictable, measurable degree of *in*accuracy.

Now many physicists are dissatisfied with these theories and consider them mere stopgaps. Statistical methods, Bridgman observes, are generally used either to conceal vast ignorance or to simplify vast confusion. Such messy, haphazard behavior of electrons distresses men brought up on law and order; they accordingly look forward to a day when subtler legislation will again induce all the electrons to keep their appointments like little gentlemen. For what is involved here is the fundamental principle of causation. Some physicists regard the surrender of strict causal laws as a threat to the integrity, even the possibility of science. Others agree with Erwin Schroedinger, that cause-and-effect is mere "mechanico-morphism" and should be scrapped with other primitive habits of thought. Still others, such as Einstein and Planck, occupy the middle ground, believing that the traditional formulation of the causal principle is rough and superficial, but that the principle itself is still indispensable to science.

In the face of such distinguished disagreement, it would be brash of a layman to settle the issue. Yet he may wonder whether the concept of cause actually has been given up; the very physicists who argue against it say that we must give it up *because* of such and such facts. What is under fire, at any rate, appears to be only a particular kind of causation, the mechanical concept of classical physics. This was an outgrowth of the common-sense notion of cause as an external force—a notion rooted in our own experience of pushing and pulling, which W. H. George describes as "the triumph of muscle over mind." (Thus the peasant to whom the steam engine was explained asked to see the horse that pulled the locomotive.) The point of the new concepts in physics, however, is that gravitation, for instance, is not a physical something that *makes* apples fall. It is a formula, a concise way of saying that all apples *do* fall, and of linking this fact with other regular sequences. Cause-and-effect may therefore be considered a tautology, a restatement of the observed correlations and uniformities in nature. But however they are described, the important thing is that we can and do make out uniform sequences. The Principle of Indeterminacy applies only to our present *descriptions* of what goes on inside the atom, sets a limit to our possible observation. It does not necessarily apply to the *behavior* of the atom, much less of the stars, or destroy the fundamental assumption of continuity. Whatever they think, in their actual operations physicists continue to bank on continuity and regularity.

Hence the layman may safely leave this problem to the experts. It is significant and healthy that such questions are being raised, in view of all the "necessities of thought" that have unnecessarily hampered it, and the answer to questions so stated will not seriously affect the nature of our knowledge as it is now conceived. Whatever strict causal laws may be invented will for the physicists still be working hypotheses, not final truths. "As a matter of fact," wrote Max Planck, "we have no means whatsoever of proving or disproving the existence of causation in the external world of nature." And in any event the causes assigned are always relative and arbitrary, not absolute and complete, for they never have a beginning or end. The scientist stops at some point, behind which one can always go in search of still larger or deeper causes—the cause, say, of gravitation. Thus John Smith explains a noise by saying that little Willie just smashed a plate, and he disposes of the problem by spanking Willie. He could also make this cause the beginning of an endless analysis, leading through the laws of sound and the psychology of Willie to the whole content of human knowledge, the whole history of the human race. Any single event involves the entire system in which it takes place. Finally one is asking, what is the "cause" of the universe?

Strictly, such questions are meaningless; and they have tormented men for ages. If nature abhors a vacuum, then men are indeed children of nature. They must somehow fill in all the empty spaces in their picture of the world—just as the anguished Victorians could not bear the sight of a blank wall and cluttered up their rooms with bric-a-brac. The idea of an infinite, eternal universe has always troubled them, for they must have a beginning and an end; the idea of a finite universe has troubled them no less, for it leaves the imponderable emptiness beyond the borders of space and before the beginning of time. They then try to explain the inexplicable by giving it a capitalized name—the First Cause, the Prime Mover, Fate, God. Somehow they must provide a mechanism, find a reason why, justify or dignify what simply *is*. And modern science is distinguished by the calm acceptance of empty spaces, the calm awareness of the meaningless question —with the realization that to call a question meaningless is to make a significant statement about nature and the operations of the human mind. "What?" and "Why?" may stimulate scientific research, but they do not, strictly, constitute its subject matter. Its spirit is a thorough-going pragmatism.

This attitude results in part from the assumption that process and energy, not matter, is the fundamental fact; if one thinks of existence as activity rather than being, he is less likely to ask how the universe "came into being." But it results as well from the realization that pure reason cannot take us to the heart of reality. If all flubjubs are dingbats and this is a flubjub, then it must also be a dingbat. This syllogism, Ogden and Richards point out, carries absolute conviction; but it proves nothing about the existence of dingbats. Formal logic can never prove the truth of its premises. Man can never be certain that his logic is the logic of things, that the scheme of science represents nature completely and represents nothing else. For all human purposes man is in fact the measure of the universe; but nobody knows exactly what it is he is measuring. In the past, scientists forced on nature the limitations of the human mind, identifying their picture of reality with reality itself. Now physicists recognize that this was but a subtler form of the ancient anthropomorphic habit; man was simply creating nature in his own image. So, indeed, he must if he is to deal with it at all. But for efficient dealings he must also be aware of what he is doing.

This article makes a key distinction between attitudes of modern and traditional scientists by using the phrase "human standpoint." You are, of course, no modern scientist; yet you have recently concluded an activity—measuring the wind—that was at least faintly scientific, and you are after all as modern a person as any scientist. What about *your* "human standpoint"? As you think over your experience with your anemometer in essay 13, can you see yourself as limited by a human standpoint that is finally "anthropomorphic" in Muller's sense?

To answer this question, you might begin by addressing yourself to several other questions that can be made up from the phraseology of Muller's article. "Strictly," he says (page 178), "physicists do not know what they are talking about." Is there a way in which you can see yourself as not knowing what you were talking about in essay 13—an ignorance that had nothing to do with the crudity of your instrument or your innocence about meteorology? What does "strictly" mean here? Again (same paragraph): "They do not so much uncover truth as create it." Were you in any way a creator of truth? Muller's emphasis is on "the act of the observer as the essence of the situation." Can your situation be seen in that way, so that your act of observing becomes its "essence"? Implied in such a discussion is a special meaning of "truth"—that is, as something not "uncovered" but "created." Can an appropriate definition of *wind* be proposed in similar terms, and on the basis of your own experience with wind in essay 13?

Directions for Essay 14

Resee your experience with your anemometer (essay 13) by reconsidering and analyzing it in the light of the "human standpoint" of Muller's article. Conclude your analysis with a careful definition of "wind"—a definition that is directly related to the theme you have just composed.

Chapter
15
The Writer's Art

The article that follows is by the late distinguished Harvard physicist who has already been referred to in this book—P. W. Bridgman. Some of the statements made by Muller in chapter 14 about the revolution in physics you will now find corroborated by a genuine physicist talking about his trade. This article is a summary of an address Mr. Bridgman gave to an academic society in Boston. It is not easy reading, but if you find yourself in difficulties it may be sobering to remember that an educated audience was expected to follow it as delivered orally to them a single time.

Your problem in this final assignment is to relate some of Bridgman's terms in this address to problems you have experienced in this course of exercises, or in other words to find a parallel between the modern physicist's situation and your own as a writer, a composer of essays.

Philosophical Implications of Physics

P. W. BRIDGMAN

It is common knowledge that since the turn of the century the physicist has passed through what amounts to an intellectual crisis forced by the discovery of experimental facts of a sort which he had not previously envisaged, and which he would not even have thought possible. These new facts were in the first instance in the realm of relativity phenomena, and only later in the quantum realm. It was the relativity phenomena, that is, the phenomena in the realms of high velocities, that had the chief influence in modifying the conceptual outlook of the physicist. Some of these effects were highly paradoxical, and included such effects as meter sticks whose length changed when they were set in motion, clocks which ran slow when moving, and weights which became heavier when moving. In fact, these effects were so paradoxical and contrary to common sense that some physicists and most men in the street refused to accept them and even sought to throw them out of court by ridicule. But the facts refused to be thrown out of court, and the paradoxes were presently resolved by Einstein's theory of relativity. This theory embraced in the first place the mathematical theory by which all the facts were correlated into a single mathematical structure. But no less notable as an intellectual achievement and equally essential to the removal of paradox was Einstein's handling of the physical concepts which entered the mathematical edifice. It is this latter which is our concern this evening. There were two aspects to Einstein's handling of the physical concepts. There

From the American Academy of Arts and Sciences *Bulletin* 3, no. 5 (February 1950). Reprinted by permission of the Academy and the author.

was in the first place a realization that the paradoxes involved primarily questions of meaning and that the common sense meanings of the physical terms such as length and time were not sharp enough to serve in the new physical situations. In the second place there was the method by which the necessary increased sharpness was imparted to meanings. This method was to specify the operations which were involved in concrete instances in applying the term whose meaning is in question.

The attitude toward meanings which eliminated the paradoxes of relativity theory has been carried over by the physicist into all the rest of physics, particularly into the new realm of quantum phenomena, where it is absolutely essential to any valid thinking at all. The physicist has come to see that the common sense meanings of many of his terms as he has adapted them from the daily life of common sense are not precise nor unique, but are really multiple and apply to a number of different procedures. . . .

The technique by which the physicist makes himself conscious of the multiple meanings of many of his terms is a technique which can be carried over with profit into the situations of daily life. This technique we have seen consists of an analysis of the operations which are used in applying the term in concrete instances. If it should turn out that different operations are used in different circumstances to define what is ostensibly the same term, then precision in the use of language demands that we should recognize the difference by inventing new terms to cover the recognizably different operations. It will turn out on examination that nearly all our abstract terms have multiple meanings. For instance, "democracy" as used by a Russian does not have the same meaning as when used by an American. The reason that it does not have the same meaning is that what the Russian does to determine whether a given society is democratic is not the same as what the American does. The Russian asks whether on election day any citizen may go to the polls and mark a cross opposite the only name on the ballot, a name which was placed there by the single party which directs the affairs of the country. The American on the other hand asks whether on election day the citizen may go to the polls and mark a cross opposite his choice of several names on the ballot, which were placed there by one or the other of several parties, in one of which he himself may have played a role in selecting the name. Since the operations for determining whether a given society is a democracy or not are different, the meaning of the term itself is different, and properly two different words should be used. The retention of a single term leads only to confusion, a confusion which may be willfully cultivated by those who can profit by it.

A consciousness of the presumptive inadequacy of the common terms which are the unthinking intellectual legacy of the race should be continually with us, and should impart a definite bias to all the thinking of a modern man. In fact, it seems to me that no one should feel himself educated until he has acquired this bias, and one of the primary objects of a truly liberal education should be to impart it.

Suppose now that my proselytizing has been effective enough to make a man embark on an operational analysis of his meanings, what is involved? He will obviously need to be able to specify what the operations are that he uses to give his meanings. He will find almost at once that there are different sorts of operation—operations on different levels. Let us consider first the operations of the physicist. To be specific, what are the operations by which he gives meaning to "length"? We need not go into full detail here, but it is obvious that his is an operation of measurement, and as such it is performed with a certain instrument, in this case a meter stick. We may, then, recognize in general a level of instrumental operations or laboratory operations. But it is obvious that the operation of measuring a length is not exclusively an operation with the meter stick, because we have to count the number of times the meter stick is applied, and the operation of counting is one that we do in our heads and not with an instrument, although perhaps we could. We recognize, therefore, another great class of operations beside the instrumental, namely mental operations. I believe that examination would disclose that the meanings of the larger part of the terms which the physicist uses are to be found in mental operations. This I believe to be true in even greater degree of the terms of daily life. Comparatively few of these terms find their meanings through simple direct "objective" operations in the "external" world in the way that the instrumental operations of the physicist find their meaning. Of the terms that do thus find their meaning the best examples are the names of things, such as "cat" or "tree." But abstract nouns find their meanings through operations which are almost exclusively mental. These mental operations, furthermore, are in large degree of a special type which are not especially important for the physicist, namely verbal operations. Verbal operations are a particular sort of verbal behavior. Verbal behavior is such a universal characteristic of man that it must be recognized that he has a verbal as well as a physical environment. In this verbal environment complex patterns of behavior occur, which for any individual in a given culture may have all the appearance of compulsion and inevitability that the patterns forced on him by his external objective environment do. Corresponding to this verbal compulsion and inevitability, verbal operations are possible which may be performed with as little uncertainty as the operations of the physical world.

What now is the significance of a term whose meaning has thus been fixed in terms of verbal operations? I think it is obvious that it may have varying kinds and degrees of significance. In the first place, man's verbal environment is a product of evolution continually subject to the restriction that it have survival value, so that the presumption is that there is a fairly good correspondence between the verbal world and the physical world. It follows that one may make experiments in the verbal environment and then transfer the results of these experiments to the physical environment with rather good prospects of success. It is, I think, a rather common human trait to deal with the physical environment in such a verbal fashion; it is more likely to be the method the more novel or unfamiliar the physical situation. Observation inclines me to the belief that it is the method by which many women deal with mechanical situations. But I believe that it will be conceded that it is less satisfactory than more direct methods.

It is, I think, the tacit implication in most language that eventually meanings can be made to emerge from the verbal environment and make connection with something more concrete and physical, and our verbal usages are based on this presupposition. In many cases, however, explicit analysis has not been made to find whether such nonverbal emergence can in fact be made to occur. When the analysis is made, I believe it will often be found, particularly with regard to abstract terms, that such emergence does not occur. It is not surprising that this should be the case, because the evolution of our abstract terms has been subject to no such drastic survival criterion as have our commoner terms, but they have often been subject only to the requirement that they produce in our fellows the reaction that we want. Since this reaction is in many cases merely some specific social behavior, words get fastened in language without necessarily having any objective physical reference. This is particularly the case if the social behavior which it was intended to evoke by the use of the word is itself merely verbal behavior. This is the case in many, perhaps most, of our social situations. Everyone is predisposed to it by the character of our elementary education, for usually the only check which is applied to a child to find whether he has grasped an idea or caught a meaning is to see whether he makes the proper verbal reaction.

It seems to me that a man is not properly educated to grapple with the problems of our age unless he understands at least two things about his verbal environment. The first is the extreme complexity of the verbal structure which man has erected. Man has always been the builder: of verbal structures no less than of pyramids and great walls of China. Within this verbal environment it is possible for people to live together with agreement, each member of society acting according to patterns of behavior which his neighbor can predict. Often the ability to be able to predict verbal behavior is the only criterion imposed for a satisfactory verbalism, and the fact that it satisfies this criterion is no guarantee that it will have validity in the external physical world, although many verbalisms do have such physical validity. The second thing which I believe that a modern man must have to be educated to cope with his verbal environment is a knowledge of the results of an operational analysis of the important abstract terms used by the culture in which he lives. It is particularly important that he know what terms are capable of eventual emergence into the "objective," or physical, and those which are not capable of such eventual emergence but find their meaning only in terms of a regress which never leaves the verbal level. In other words, it is important that he know where are the open verbal chains. I believe that it will be found that these open verbal chains are much commoner than a complacent humanity likes to believe.

The operational attitude toward meanings is only one aspect of the operational point of view in general. This is to see the world in terms of activities rather than in terms of things. If one adopts this point of view, then much of what we have been saying about meanings becomes tautological, for meanings under this point of view would automatically be expressed in terms of some sort of activity, that is, some sort of operation. The significance of the operational attitude toward meanings then is to be found in the analysis into specific operations in concrete cases, for our experience then enables us to judge whether the specific operations are of value for the purposes we have in mind.

Common sense analyzes the world into objects which in greater or less degree are endowed with stability and permanence. Common sense accepts this analysis for its purposes as an ultimate analysis, and treats its objects as the ultimate components of "reality." Now this is no reproach to common sense, because every analysis has to stop somewhere, because of the finite duration of human life if for no other reason. The only question we have to ask with regard to any specific restricted analysis is whether it goes far enough to meet the demands that we shall put upon it.

It is true that for most of the purposes of daily life we do not need to analyze beyond the concept of object, but this is by no means the situation in the new realm of quantum phenomena which experiment has opened to the physicist. Here the common-sense notions of object completely fail us; there is no permanence or stability, experiments cannot be exactly repeated, measurements cannot be made in the conventional way, the very attribute of identity, which is perhaps the ultimate criterion of an object, becomes meaningless. Although we cannot deal with such situations by the methods of common sense, we are perforce constrained to deal with them as best we can and not ignore them defeatistly. What is more, the theoretical physicist has worked out a way of handling these situations which is highly satisfactory, as shown by the range of new phenomena which he has got under control. This method involves an analysis into activities, and most of these activities are in the paper-and-pencil domain and involve the manipulations of mathematical symbols according to rules many of which were evolved to meet the occasion.

Taken altogether, it seems to me that it is a simple matter of observation that an analysis of the world about us into activities goes beyond an analysis into objects. Furthermore, at the present epoch, an analysis into activities is adequate for the purposes of the physicist and as far as I can judge for the purposes of other natural scientists as well. Whether the poet and the artist would accept it as adequate in their domain I cannot pretend to say; but this is perhaps of little moment, because the poet and the artist, insofar as they are concerned with creating and not with philosophizing about what they are creating, have little traffic with analysis. The point of view which sees the world in terms of activity is closely related to the philosophical point of view set forth in the recent book by Dewey and Bentley entitled *Knowing and the Known*. . . .

It seems to me that our attitude toward many social institutions will be essentially modified if we see the world as activity. Consider for example the state and our attitude toward it. Viewed as activity, it will be impossible to think of the state as some super thing or even super person with an existence of its own. For analysis of what happens whenever we are concerned with any functioning of the state discloses that we are always concerned with the activities of individuals. Every law of the state has originated in one way or another in the actions of individuals—in a democracy by the majority vote of the individual members of a legislature, or in a dictatorship by the decree of the individual who is dictator. If I violate the law, I may be arrested by the order of some individual police captain to this or that policeman to go to my house and compel me by the display of superior force to come with him. And if I am tried and condemned, it is by some individual judge who decides by his own individual judgment what interpretation should be put upon the laws inscribed on the statute books when applied to my particular case. There is no mechanism by which the state functions except through the activities of individuals.

It may seem to many that such a realistic attitude can lead only to anarchy and chaos, and it must be admitted that there is such danger in the process of transition. But it seems to me that on the other hand it is only by adopting such a realistic view that we can hope for the development of that new ethics for which the present need is so crying and obvious, a need so new that none of the great traditional systems of ethics have adequately anticipated it.

Finally, I come to what it seems to me may well be from the long-range point of view the most revolutionary of the insights to be derived from our recent experiences in physics, more revolutionary than the insights afforded by the discoveries of Galileo and Newton or of Darwin. This is the insight that it is impossible to transcend the human reference point. The history of much of philosophy and most of religion has been the history of the attempt of the human race to transcend its own reference point by the invention of essences and absolutes and realities and existences. It should have been obvious enough, even without the experience of recent physics, that this was an impossible attempt. For even the mystic, convinced of direct communication between his soul and some supernatural external reality, would have had to admit that it was his soul, and therefore a human soul, that had the experience, and that the experience took place in his consciousness, and therefore a human consciousness. But considerations like these are so obvious that it is easy to overlook their significance. Recent experience in physics documents in another way the conclusion that it is impossible to transcend the human reference point, and by the emphasis of novelty may perhaps succeed in injecting this insight into the backbone of humanity. The new insight comes from a realization that the structure of nature may eventually be such that our processes of thought do not correspond to it sufficiently to permit us to think about it at all. We have already had an intimation of this in the behavior of very small things in the quantum domain. We have seen that in this domain there are no longer things, in the sense that a thing has individuality and identity and recurs in experience. I can conceive of no more fundamental need of thought than the need for identity and recurrence. Memory would be impossible without the background that identifies what is occurring in our minds now with something that has happened before. No operational analysis would be possible if we could not identify our operations. Without identification our mental activities would be as amorphous as we imagine must be the first experiences of a baby just born, or perhaps rather considerably unborn. The structure of nature in the direction of the very small is simply not the same as the structure of our thought; and, being so, it is meaningless even to attempt to formulate what it is like.

Similarly we meet a possible incompatibility between the structure of nature and our thought in the direction of the very large. This emergency is not yet actually upon us, but the possibility can be seen around the next corner. If the giant telescope at Palomar should indicate that the universe does not fade out but is open in the direction of the very large, we are going to be seriously embarrassed to find the proper way of thinking about it. The reason is that it is fundamental to all our theoretical thinking in physics to be able to divide the universe into two parts, one the part under investigation, and the other the rest of the universe, which is the seat of the observer but otherwise neutral. If the universe is actually open, it will not be legitimate to think of the rest of the universe as neutral, and we will lose the basis for the most sweeping generalizations that we have—the conservation of energy and the inexorable increase of entropy.

There may be differences of opinion about the seriousness of the intellectual dilemma that may be waiting for us in the direction of the very large, but there can be no difference of opinion with regard to the dilemma that now confronts us in the direction of the very small. We are now approaching a bound beyond which we are forever estopped from pushing our inquiries, not by the construction of the world, but by the construction of ourselves. The world fades out and eludes us because it becomes meaningless. We cannot even express this in the way we would like. We cannot say that there exists a world beyond any knowledge possible to us because of the nature of knowledge. The very concept of existence becomes meaningless. It is literally true that the only way of reacting to this is to shut up. We are confronted with something truly ineffable. We have reached the limit of the vision of the great pioneers of science, the vision, namely, that we live in a sympathetic world, in that it is comprehensible by our minds.

It seems to me that the impact of a realization of this will be more momentous than was ever the impact of the vision of Newton or Darwin.

Your object in essay 15 is to try applying some of these statements about problems in modern physics to your own problems as a writer. To do this we will concentrate on a few sentences from Bridgman's address:

Finally, I come to what seems to me may well be from the long-range point of view the most revolutionary of the insights to be derived from our recent experiments in physics, more revolutionary than the insights afforded by the discoveries of Galileo and Newton, or Darwin. This is the insight that it is impossible to transcend the human reference point. . . . The new insight comes from a realization that the structure of nature may eventually be such that our processes of thought do not correspond to it sufficiently to permit us to think about it at all. . . . We are now approaching a bound beyond which we are forever estopped from pushing our inquiries, not by the construction of the world, but by the construction of ourselves. The world fades out and eludes us because it becomes meaningless. We cannot even express this in the way we would like. We cannot say that there exists a world beyond any knowledge possible to us because of the nature of knowledge. It is literally true that the only way of reacting to this is to shut up. We are confronted with something truly ineffable. We have reached the limit of vision of the great pioneers of science, the vision, namely, that we live in a sympathetic world, in that it is comprehensible by our minds.

Your final theme assignment now asks you to relate some of Bridgman's terms to your own efforts at seeing and saying. You may not be a physicist at the frontiers of science, but you are (or should be) at the frontiers of your own means of expression. You too have a "human reference point" you cannot transcend; this assignment asks you to determine where that point is.

Directions for Essay 15

Select and describe a particular experience of yours as a writer of these themes, in which you felt stopped (or "estopped") from pushing your inquiries further. Explain what you were trying to do, and try to point out just where, how, and why you were stopped. Make what use you can of Bridgman's terms, such as "the human reference point," "the construction of the world," and "the construction of ourselves." What means if any do you have at your disposal, as a writer, to confront a world that is not sympathetic in that it is not comprehensible to your mind? Do you shut up? Why or why not? Conclude with a final statement on the nature of the writer's art as you have experienced it in these exercises.

Perhaps you can see from the following poem by Robert Frost that your "final statement" need not be a negative one.

For Once, Then, Something

ROBERT FROST

Others taunt me with having knelt at well-curbs
Always wrong to the light, so never seeing
Deeper down in the well than where the water
Gives me back in a shining surface picture
Me myself in the summer heaven godlike
Looking out of a wreath of fern and cloud-puffs.
Once, when trying with chin against a well-curb,

I discerned, as I thought, beyond the picture,
Through the picture, a something white, uncertain,
Something more of the depths—and then I lost it.
Water came to rebuke the too clear water.
One drop fell from a fern, and lo, a ripple
Shook whatever it was lay there at bottom,
Blurred it, blotted it out. What was that whiteness?
Truth? A pebble of quartz? For once, then, something.